PRAYI THE LECTIONARY

Prayers and Reflections for Every Week's Readings

James Woodward

and

Leslie Houlden

First published in Great Britain in 2007

Society for Promoting Christian Knowledge
36 Causton Street
London SW1P 4ST

British Library Cataloguing-in-Publication Data
A catalogue record for this book is available from the British Library

ISBN-13: 978-0-281-05854-9
ISBN-10: 0-281-05854-7

1 3 5 7 9 10 8 6 4 2

Designed and typeset by Kenneth Burnley, Wirral, Cheshire
Printed in Great Britain by Ashford Colour Press

INTRODUCTION

The readings at the Eucharist go past in a few minutes, one after another, and how many of the hearers can recall much about them by the time the service is ended? It seems a waste, and it feels sometimes that they are just a symbol of our need and duty to listen to the scriptures. There are ways of improving things. The sermon that follows them is, of course, the first weapon – but the preacher can scarcely focus on all the readings and may have a particular message to give to which a biblical passage is only loosely related. And alas, even the sermon may not survive long in the memory. What can be done to give the scripture readings a longer life for their hearers and a deeper effect on their minds?

Some churches use standard sheets, provided centrally, that give, among much else, some comments on the readings. But many parishes prefer to communicate in a way that is more tailor made to their own lives. They provide their own 'pew sheet' or 'Sunday bulletin', which will often include brief comments designed to point up the readings. These can be read at any time, publicly or privately, and can also be taken home to foster reflection and prayer.

In this book, based on the experience of one parish, we provide such material for each Sunday and other Holy Days in the three-year cycle. For each reading we give a brief comment and then bullet-points directing us to prayer. The hope is that their scale and character may be of service to other parishes that feel in need of such a resource and to individuals for prayer and reflection.

It is worth mentioning that the scripture passages correspond to those given full exposition in the three volumes of *A Scripture Commentary* (edited by Leslie Houlden and John Rogerson, SPCK), providing, like the present book, for the three years of the *Common Worship* Lectionary.

FIRST SUNDAY OF ADVENT

ISAIAH 2.1–5

We are given a familiar and vivid image of how God's 'power' works. It is the force of love and peace.

ROMANS 13.11–14

Paul tells powerfully of his sense of the pressing urgency of God's purpose – a future of light and clarity, no longer a time for the dullness of sleep, but rather the lively energy of a new day.

MATTHEW 24.36–44

God's purposes go beyond what we can expect or imagine – for ourselves and for the world in general. So we have to be alert and to hand ourselves over to him as his willing agents.

- *Where God is concerned, can we learn to 'think big'? The opposite leads to paltry results and a feeble sense of his reality.*

- *So great and so desirable is God's hope for us that to put off its being realized is both sad and foolish.*

- *Can we be ready and expectant – twin states of heart that open God's door?*

SECOND SUNDAY OF ADVENT

ISAIAH 11.1–10

We are given a picture of God's future gift of a new leader for his people. Christians saw it is a portrait of Jesus, the bringer of 'righteousness' (i.e. the justice of God). But notice, the gifts of God's Spirit in verse 2 are conveyed to us in the words of the Confirmation Service where we are taken to be one with Christ himself.

ROMANS 15.4–13

Christ sprang from Israel, but his role was universal in scope. Paul was the first to proclaim this vital insight with all clarity and to follow it up in real life.

MATTHEW 3.1–12

John the Baptist is an Advent figure because he is a symbol of expectancy looking only to what is greater than himself and to the One who is to come.

- *Pray not to lose the precious sense of expectancy for the 'more' that God will both give to us and ask of us.*

- *It has never been easy to give reality to Christ's being God-to-all. Do we yet succeed?*

- *How many-sided is the work of God's Spirit within us?*

THIRD SUNDAY OF ADVENT

ISAIAH 35.1–10

The prophet's vision of a better future is naturally rural in its imagery, but, more deeply, it is about the curing of our ills (which remain pestilential to us all). Jesus picked this vision up and made it his own.

JAMES 5.7–10

Patience with God is hard when things stand still or even get worse. But there is no wholesome alternative. To lose heart is the road to death.

MATTHEW 11.2–11

Jesus gives to John the Baptist the highest honour; yet his role was to prepare the way. The best was still to come.

- *To lose the sense of a greater future at God's hand is to admit defeat; and to stand still is to slip back.*

- *Give thanks for the constant surprise of God's love.*

- *Pray to be ready for the 'more' that God has in store.*

FOURTH SUNDAY OF ADVENT

ISAIAH 7.10–16

The passage foretells a birth, perhaps of an heir to the king. Christians seized on it and saw in it the validating of Christ as 'God-with-us'. It rang true, and had done its job.

ROMANS 1.1–7

Paul opens his letter in typical fashion. He gives his credentials (he is Christ's true agent) and sums up the message of salvation in his characteristic language.

MATTHEW 1.18–25

It is doubtful whether Matthew was much interested in the possible oddities of biology. Rather, his concern was to make sure that we realize that Jesus is truly God's gift of himself to us, purely and simply, whatever it takes.

- *Credentials and background are important – but how important?*
- *If Jesus is God-with-us, what does that tell us about God? What do we see through the window?*
- *Pray to look to Jesus, frail-yet-mighty One, who shows God to us.*

CHRISTMAS DAY AND
EVENING OF CHRISTMAS EVE

ISAIAH 9.2-7
OR ISAIAH 62.6-12 OR ISAIAH 52.7-10

These prophecies speak with joy and hope of a future in store from God. We can feel the force of their words: the best is still to come.

TITUS 2.11-14
OR TITUS 3.4-7 OR HEBREWS 1.1-4 (5-12)

God's gift of himself in Jesus, long promised, is for the good of everyone.

LUKE 2.1-14 (15-20)
OR LUKE 2.1-7 (8-20) OR JOHN 1.1-14

Whether we hear the truth in the form of the story or in more abstract words, we are to combine the simplicity and the wonder of God's gift. It is universal in its scope and purpose.

- *We praise God for the gift of Jesus: let us adore him.*
- *Pray to feel the wonder of God's simplicity of love.*
- *We long to deepen our love of God – for his own sake.*

FIRST SUNDAY OF CHRISTMAS

ISAIAH 63.7–9

Isaiah sees all the difference between sending a messenger and coming in person. Christians have always felt that difference and believed that, in Christ, God had bridged the gap.

HEBREWS 2.10–18

The writer makes much of Jesus, one of us, as the pioneer of God's purposes. It is a special version of the gospel message – and an encouraging way of putting it. It gives great hope, yet leaves the future open ended. We must not close off God's options.

MATTHEW 2.13–23

This dark and terrible story illustrates a mysterious theme of the Bible (and indeed of life). Only through loss and suffering does great good come about. We would prefer things otherwise, but we can see darkly that we should not put immediate profit at the heart of our being.

- *God bridges the gap between himself and us. Can we bear to receive his gesture of love?*

- *Jesus leads from the front: can we bear to follow?*

- *The necessary darkness, as it seems, can make it hard for us to 'see the light'. Is that wise or fair of us?*

SECOND SUNDAY OF CHRISTMAS

JEREMIAH 31.7–14

God's purposes, full of blessing, call out of us the most joyful response we are capable of.

OR ECCLESIASTICUS 24.1–12

'Wisdom' was a symbol for God's loving purpose for his people: meaning that it was not frivolous or in the least irrational, but full of depth and sense.

EPHESIANS 1.3–14

We read a long and fulsome utterance of praise to God for his gift of Christ – for our great good.

JOHN 1.(1–9), 10–18

In Jesus, vivid in what the Gospels tell of him, we see God in the shape and setting of human life. We observe, imagine and we give thanks.

- *Praise God for his gift of himself to us in the life of Jesus.*

- *Pray for grace to see, to learn and to follow.*

- *Give thanks to God for all creation, laid out before us.*

THE EPIPHANY

ISAIAH 60.1–6

In the later Old Testament writings there is a turning of the eyes to the outside world with a growing sense of other nations' place in God's purposes and of Israel's benevolent role towards them.

EPHESIANS 3.1–12

The apostle Paul's great achievement was to see Christ as God's gift for all, Jews and gentiles alike, and both on the same footing. By making it unnecessary to become a Jew as a step to Christian conversion, he opened the door wide for the future of Christianity.

MATTHEW 2.1–12

The visit of the Magi, gentile astrologers from afar, foreshadows beautifully in Jesus' infancy the future boundless scope of his sway over the hearts and minds of humanity.

- *It is hard to be truly universal in spirit and in welcome. Pray for openness of heart.*

- *Paul's leap of faith was so clear sighted and brave as to take our breath away.*

- *Reflect on the beautiful simplicity of Christ to be venerated even by those of complex and sophisticated minds.*

THE BAPTISM OF CHRIST
(FIRST SUNDAY OF EPIPHANY)

ISAIAH 42.1–9

We may read this passage as a picture of the ministry of Jesus – marked by both gentleness and power, by healing and the establishment of liberty and justice.

ACTS 10.34–43

Peter makes a momentous move. Jesus' message and work were not confined to Jews but were for people of every race and kind.

MATTHEW 3.13–17

In an act of humility, the baptism of Jesus makes clear who he is – the chosen one of God who will fulfil his purposes.

- *Can we share the excitement of the prophet's hope?*
- *Pray that your faith might include people of all kinds.*
- *Reflect on the simple wonder of the role of Jesus on God's behalf.*

SECOND SUNDAY OF EPIPHANY

ISAIAH 49.1–7

As so often in the later chapters of Isaiah, the prophet's message is one of generous openness to human beings in general in the name of Israel's God, now seen as everyone's God.

1 CORINTHIANS 1.1–9

Paul writes to a congregation he himself had gathered, and he proudly states his position as apostle (or agent) of Christ towards them. 'Saints' here means 'belonging to God', and the later sense of 'especially holy' lay in the future. To be Christians, whoever we are, is to stand on holy ground, where God is to be found.

JOHN 1.29–42

Here, John the Baptist recognizes Jesus as God's chosen one, with the Spirit to validate him; and without delay Jesus recruits followers to his cause.

- *Pray to share the breadth of vision shown by the prophet.*
- *To be 'holy' is first and foremost to know oneself to be living in true relationship to God.*
- *Jesus is 'Lamb of God'. Sacrifice is always on the cards, for him – and for us who are his.*

THIRD SUNDAY OF EPIPHANY

ISAIAH 9.1–4

Looking beyond Israel's bounds, Isaiah sees the shining of God's joyful light, bringing an end to oppression.

1 CORINTHIANS 1.10–18

Hero-worship and squabbles in the congregation enfeeble Christian life, and Paul hates it. His remedy rests on Jesus' death as the sole source of power and alone worthy of loyalty.

MATTHEW 4.12–23

The evangelist picks up the passage from Isaiah, as he looks to the spread of the good news; and he makes that point here, as the story of Jesus' ministry begins: he summons disciples and he relieves distress.

- *We must trust that the faith can be a force of liberation for all kinds of slaves and victims.*

- *Bickering usually makes for weakness, but in a Christian group it is more: it is a perversion of the gospel.*

- *We should reflect on the basic simplicity of Jesus' call and, we trust, our response.*

FOURTH SUNDAY OF EPIPHANY

1 KINGS 17.8-16

Elijah, man of God, brings life-saving aid to a poor widow and she is a gentile, beyond his formal sphere of charity.

1 CORINTHIANS 1.18-31

Paul plays with the idea of 'wisdom'. Some in the Church boast of their religious depth. Paul brushes that aside. God's wisdom is to be seen in the weakness of Christ crucified.

JOHN 2.1-11

John probably relates this story to say that Jewish faith ('water') has now found its rich and abundant fulfilment in Christ ('wine').

- *How wide are we ready to let our generosity extend?*
- *We must return to the strange simplicity of true religion, shaming our clever discussion.*
- *Can we tell when being convinced of our own faith leads us to dismiss the truths in the faith of others?*

THE PRESENTATION OF CHRIST

(2 FEBRUARY)

MALACHI 3.1–5

The focus is on the Temple in Jerusalem, symbol of God's presence. Malachi sees it as the scene of the coming revelation of God's power.

HEBREWS 2.14–18

Hebrews is firm on Christ's genuine humanity. This is what enables us to see him as truly 'one of us' – and enables him to be our representative before God – just like the high priest in the Temple of old.

LUKE 2.22–40

Luke tells of Mary's humble keeping of the Jewish law relating to childbirth. As the new world is born, the old is superseded but not despised.

- *We need powerful symbols, like the Temple in Malachi's prophecy. How powerful can we let them be, and can they come to dominate the reality they stand for?*

- *It is surely helpful to see Jesus as our 'go-between' in relation to God. He has a foot on either side and joins the two together.*

- *Religious devotion can be glad of the past, even as the future dawns and draws our eyes.*

FIFTH SUNDAY OF EPIPHANY

ISAIAH 58.1-9A (9B-12)

Religious observance always runs the risk of being complacent and superficial: but true relationship with God is made of sterner stuff.

1 CORINTHIANS 2.1-12 (13-16)

Paul strives to get his converts to see the true depth of what he tries to bring them: no human theory-making, but the reality of God's truth.

MATTHEW 5.13-20

We are called to the highest possible level of service to God. Only then can we hope to affect the life of society at large.

- *May we always seek the depth of God's love.*
- *Pray to be ardent in the quest for God.*
- *We trust in God's enabling power in our discipleship.*

SIXTH SUNDAY OF EPIPHANY

DEUTERONOMY 30.15–20

God sets before Israel the stark choice as the land lies before them: to live by his law or to reject it – with inevitable results either way.

OR ECCLESIASTICUS 15.15–20

The writer of this book is a clear-sighted servant of God, and he sees the plain choices that face his people: to obey or to reject.

1 CORINTHIANS 3.1–9

The Christians in Corinth are apt to bicker and divide – here, in hero-worshipping various teachers and leaders of the Church. This distracts from the fact that their roots are in Christ alone.

MATTHEW 5.21–37

Jesus is shown penetrating to the depths of traditional rules. Only so can their full meaning be seen.

- *Pray not to shirk hard choices in loyalties or actions.*

- *May we preserve at all costs our unity in Christ.*

- *Let us never be content with merely formal religion.*

SEVENTH SUNDAY OF EPIPHANY

LEVITICUS 19.1–2, 9–18

This summary of Jewish morality, even more clearly than the familiar Ten Commandments, is based in social relations under God within Israel. Worth pondering all the same, even in our very different society.

1 CORINTHIANS 3.10–11, 16–23

Paul is a mixture of awareness of his vital role as Christ's apostle and a sense that God through Christ transcends all that he does – and all that his Christians are.

MATTHEW 5.38–48

The Sermon on the Mount goes beyond conventional moral teaching, with its stress on fairness and social boundaries. Generosity and love leap all fences.

- *Pray to hold to high ideals, through all failures.*
- *May we be saved from narrowness of vision.*
- *Thank God that he raises our eyes to the highest possibilities.*

SECOND SUNDAY BEFORE LENT

GENESIS 1.1—2.3

This first of the two accounts of creation in Genesis makes a set scheme of it, stressing that all comes from God's all-powerful decree and depends utterly upon him.

ROMANS 8.18–25

Paul sees our assured hope of salvation as bringing with it the release of all creation from its appointed state.

MATTHEW 6.25–34

Jesus teaches us to live before God in the everyday world with simplicity and so without anxiety; because it is God's world and we are his, our needs can be met and we should not fret for more.

- *Give thanks to God for the wonder of his created order.*
- *Pray that we as Christians play our part in the renewal of the world.*
- *Need it be a vain hope to put worries aside, out of trust in God's love?*

SUNDAY NEXT BEFORE LENT

EXODUS 24.12–18

This passage tells of one of the key episodes in the Old Testament story. It is the occasion when God makes his solemn bond of faith with his people, and the vision of his glory seals it.

2 PETER 1.16–21

We have here the only reference outside the Gospels to the story of Jesus' Transfiguration, which the writer sees as putting the stamp of authority on Jesus' whole mission.

MATTHEW 17.1–9

A strange story which points ahead to Jesus' resurrection glory but also endorses him as in the succession to (and as greater than) Israel's two greatest spokesmen for God, Moses and Elijah.

- *We reflect on the unbreakable bond between God and ourselves, his beloved creation and his people.*
- *What do we see as signs of Jesus' authority?*
- *We thank God for giving himself so unstintingly in the person of Jesus.*

ASH WEDNESDAY

JOEL 2.1–2, 12–17

The prophet calls on God's people to observe the holy time with all solemnity. It binds all together in the strict, heartfelt service of God.

OR ISAIAH 58.1–12
God speaks via the prophet in exasperation at superficial religion. True service of God lies not in ritual acts but in care for the needy, bringing joy for all.

2 CORINTHIANS 5.20B—6.10

Paul sets out his credentials as Christ's ambassador. They lie in the trials he has endured – leading to all the many blessings of the gospel of Christ.

MATTHEW 6.1–6, 16–21

Religious observance can be done for absurd reasons, even to win the approval of other people. Purity of motive is required – for the love of God.

OR JOHN 8.1–11
We are not to sin – but equally, we must not be censorious, in effect putting ourselves on a pedestal of virtue. How wickedly foolish!

- *Pray for purity in our love of God.*
- *The gift of Lent is to deepen our true service.*
- *Thank God for the chance to grow in love.*

FIRST SUNDAY OF LENT

GENESIS 2.15–17; 3.1–7

The story is a picture of the flawed character of our human nature, however 'good' we try to be. It is a sad truth about us – but not the whole truth.

ROMANS 5.12–19

The fuller truth is that God does not abandon us to our spoiled and foolish selfishness. With Christ to stir us and Christ for us, we are taken out of ourselves to a quite different level of life. It is God's supreme, free gift.

MATTHEW 4.1–11

Jesus triumphs over the natural temptations of his mission and (unlike Adam and Eve) is not turned away from what he must be and do.

- *The fact that we are flawed must be humbly accepted if ever we are to be healed.*
- *The healing comes from God. Can we grasp it gladly?*
- *Temptations are often minor, but they can be symptoms of (and the test of) where we really stand.*

SECOND SUNDAY OF LENT

GENESIS 12.1–4A

In Abraham, the focus of the Old Testament story narrows from humanity as a whole to one man – with a huge destiny, which spreads out again, for the good of all.

ROMANS 4.1–5, 13–17

As a Jew, Paul knew Abraham as the seed of God's good will to us. To get that great boon out to the world at large, Paul seized on Abraham's faith and trust in God as the key. It is all that God requires of any of us.

JOHN 3.1–17

The final verses give the other side (God's side) of the coin from Paul. We trust, but first God gives, without stint or reserve, out of sheer love.

- *We often tend to think of the big picture (nations, humanity). Is that the best way, when great matters are at stake, or is the small scale often crucial?*

- *Can our natural pride accept that God needs only trust, and not, for example, that we earn salvation by our perhaps rather threadbare virtue?*

- *Reflect that being accepted by God – receiving the gift – is the heart of our great good.*

THIRD SUNDAY OF LENT

EXODUS 17.1–7

Trusting in God, not only in principle but through thick and thin, is often an ordeal; but faith is the better for being tested.

ROMAN 5.1–11

Paul never ceases to be amazed at God's love for us – creatures of his who, in sober fact, merit nothing from him at all.

JOHN 4.5–42

John presents Jesus under two images, and he 'plays' with both. Jesus is the giver of the 'water' (baptism?) that alone can slake our real thirst; and he is the 'place' where God is most truly worshipped, our bond with God.

- *Can we really be heartened when our faith is tested, or do we fight shy?*
- *We pray – to keep to the faith that God's love is beyond all we have a right to expect.*
- *Jesus fulfils all our good and godly hopes, whatever shape we give to them.*

FOURTH SUNDAY OF LENT

1 SAMUEL 16.1–13

Samuel the prophet and seer cannot believe that God will work through the mere young son who is chosen. God's ways are not our ways.

EPHESIANS 5.8–14

'Light' is a frequent image for God's gift – and it stands for truth, moral purity of heart and singleness of purpose.

JOHN 9.1–41

Despite all discouragement, the man wins through – to physical sight, but more: to recognition of Jesus as God's gift. It is the revolution of his life.

- *Pray for patience to discern God's real purpose.*
- *Thank God for the gift of 'sight' – perception of the true and the real.*
- *We confess how blind we can be, even to obvious good.*

MOTHERING SUNDAY

EXODUS 2.1–10

Male Hebrew babies had to be drowned in the Nile, so Moses' mother acted shrewdly to save his life. In due course, he in turn was God's agent to save his people from slavery. It is a picture of Jesus' role for us all. Salvation hangs by a (golden) thread, does it not?

OR 1 SAMUEL 1.20–28
The birth of Samuel, dedicated for God's special purpose, is an advance-echo for the coming of Jesus.

2 CORINTHIANS 1.3–7

Here we see Paul's true pastoral spirit as he writes to a Christian community that causes him much trouble.

OR COLOSSIANS 3.12–17
Here is Paul's ideal picture of the Christian community – a generous, kindly people, devoted to God's praise, all for the sake of Christ.

LUKE 2.33–35

Like the mother of Moses, Mary has a crisis ahead. Jesus will be a man at risk as well as the giver of life and freedom.

OR JOHN 19.25B–27
Jesus provides for the future in his moment of death. Perhaps we should see his mother as standing for old Israel and the beloved disciple as the Church of the future, now inaugurated.

- *Is it hard to accept that the triumph of good is never plain sailing?*

- *Is it hard for church life to live up to so attractive an ideal?*

- *Pray for grace to share Mary's pain and suffering for the ultimate good of us all.*

FIFTH SUNDAY OF LENT

(PASSIONTIDE BEGINS)

EZEKIEL 37.1–14

The dry bones stand for the people of Israel, and the prophet's vision brings assurance of their new life, restored by God's power.

ROMANS 8.6–11

God's Spirit is his life-giving power. It exemplifies his central, all-embracing character. Those who receive him will have true 'life' like the dry bones. The vision comes true.

JOHN 11.1–45

The raising of Lazarus is Jesus' greatest 'sign' told in this Gospel. It shows us his power over all enemies – and the sisters rightly come to faith.

- *What if your life is like dry bones, and where are the signs of newness?*
- *We believe that such life is God's gift, available for us.*
- *Life out of death is the gift at its most dramatic. What might it mean to us, even now?*

PALM SUNDAY

(LITURGY OF THE PASSION)

ISAIAH 50.4–9A

The passage is a haunting description of one who suffers for the cause of God. It is no wonder that Christians soon saw it as helping to make sense of what happened to Jesus, and bringing it within the scope of God's mysterious purposes.

PHILIPPIANS 2.5–11

We should probably read this passage as an early Christian hymn, summing up (rather like a kind of creed) the career of Christ: from God's highest place of esteem and dignity to the degradation of death by crucifixion, and then to glorious vindication.

MATTHEW 26.14—27.66

Matthew tells the familiar story of Jesus' arrest, trial and death, much as the earlier Gospel of Mark had done; but adding his own vivid touches, like Pilate washing his hands and leaving all responsibility to the Jewish authorities, and then Judas' suicide out of remorse.

OR MATTHEW 27.11–54

The shorter extract focuses on the climax of Pilate's trial of Jesus, his final torture and death by crucifixion – the inexorable process fills our vision.

- *Can we really believe that suffering can be beneficial and the only route to some great benefits? Here we see the principle at work on the grandest of scales.*

- *We wonder at the sweep of Christ's self-humbling and rejoice at his vindication.*

- *We should identify in imagination with characters in the story – and make what we can of ourselves.*

MAUNDY THURSDAY

EXODUS 12.1–4 (5–10), 11–14

The Last Supper was the Passover Meal, so here are the rubrics for its
observance – on the eve of Israel's great salvation from slavery in Egypt.
We have always seen it as the model for our redemption in Christ.

1 CORINTHIANS 11.23–26

The oldest telling of the story of the Last Supper, whose actions are the model
for the Eucharist – for all times and places.

JOHN 13.1–17, 31B–35

The washing of the disciples' feet is an act of deep humility, teaching the bond
of love that is to join the followers of Jesus and make them one.

- *Pray for a deeper devotion to Jesus in the Eucharist.*
- *We praise God for our rescue by God from all that threatens us.*
- *We trust that we can grow in love for each other.*

GOOD FRIDAY

ISAIAH 52.13—53.12

The so-called 'Servant Song' has been seen from early times as presaging Jesus' Passion, and it may indeed have helped to nourish his own vocation. It tells of a righteous sufferer in God's good cause.

HEBREWS 10.16–25

The writer sees Jesus as having fulfilled the purpose of Old Testament worship: to bring us near to God in purity.

OR HEBREWS 4.14–16; 5.7–9

The high priest represented all Israel before God and entered his presence on their behalf. Jesus fulfils that purpose for us all and for ever, giving us the sure access that we desire.

JOHN 18.1—19.42

The Passion according to John focuses on the trial before Pilate, with its twin themes of kingship and truth. Jesus shows himself to be the genuine article, and he dies in total fulfilment of his mission.

- *Pray to identify with Jesus in his suffering.*

- *Praise God for his love shown to us in Jesus.*

- *We rejoice in the completion of the mission of Jesus.*

EASTER DAY

ACTS 10.34-43

Peter gives a summary of the story of the salvation brought by Jesus, but the crucial point here is the universal scope of that work; it is for gentiles as well as for Jews. A major step in the Church's life and the spread of the good news.

OR JEREMIAH 31.1-6
The prophet foresees a time when Israel's hopes will be amply fulfilled, in joy and without stint.

COLOSSIANS 3.1-4

To become a Christian is to enter a whole new sphere of life, with Christ as its principle, indeed its true setting. This is the real fruit of Easter.

JOHN 20.1-18

Two stories of Easter Day, telling first of the abandoned tomb and then of Jesus' meeting with Mary Magdalene. A new world is born and the old is put behind. And love and recognition are the marks of the new.

OR MATTHEW 28.1-10
The women discover the tomb empty and report their finding – with joy and fear, both fitting reactions to the wonder of the day.

- *To contemplate the story of Jesus is itself an act of thanksgiving to God.*
- *We pray not to forget the revolution that being a Christian must mean for us.*
- *Which are the events and experiences that clinch Christian faith for us?*

SECOND SUNDAY OF EASTER

EXODUS 14.10–31; 15.20–21

The Israelites try to flee their Egyptian captors. All is in the balance: will they get away or not? With God's help, success is assured.

OR ACTS 2.14A, 22–32
This first example of apostolic preaching after the Ascension sees the raising of Jesus as fulfilling prophecy. It is meant by God and no mere fluke of nature.

1 PETER 1.3–9

An exuberant affirmation of Christian belief written to people who must be ready for their share in Christ's triumph in the long term to be tested by suffering in the short term.

JOHN 20.19–31

Should faith depend on evidence? No, says the Gospel, for that destroys the character of faith itself. Faith is a matter of pure trust. Thomas is a sobering model for us as well as a reassurance.

- *We are surely to be content that God's deep-laid providence should be worked out, for the good of all his creatures.*

- *Is it not hard to trust when the going is hard? It is also uniquely important and full of reward.*

- *Pray for the gift of pure trust, the true sign of love – not demanding proofs or measurable recompense.*

THIRD SUNDAY OF EASTER

ZEPHANIAH 3.14–20

The prophet foresees, exuberantly, a time of fulfilment when all shall be well.

OR ACTS 2.14A, 36–41

Peter's first great sermon in Jerusalem has a miraculous response, and baptism follows. Only rarely does religious activity flourish at such a high pitch. We should rejoice without depending on such striking events for faith to be valid.

1 PETER 1.17–23

We must be encouraged when we read of how Christian life felt in the days when all was fresh and new. Life in the here-and-now seems like a kind of exile from our true home with God – where, through Christ, we truly belong.

LUKE 24.13–35

The meal at Emmaus shows us 'the breaking of bread' as a key way of recognizing Jesus, ever and afresh, and as a way of learning his true significance. To walk with him through life can even be an unconscious way of 'finding' him.

- *God's Spirit is his gift to renew and remake us, and to remove scales from our eyes.*

- *Pray not to lose a sense of tension between the 'everyday world' and the 'real world' whose meaning is given by God.*

- *We should hold to a sense of the wonder of Christ-with-us in the Eucharist.*

FOURTH SUNDAY OF EASTER

GENESIS 7

Noah in his ark, surviving the direst threats, can be seen as a symbol of
salvation against all odds. In a way, we are always saved by the skin of our
teeth, by an act of grace.

OR ACTS 2.42–47

Being Christian thrives best not just on our 'going to church' or even on our
'being good', but also on some kind of shared Christian community life for the
good of all.

1 PETER 2.19–25

The message is sobering: that we are never so Christian as when, like Jesus, we
suffer undeservedly. But the outcome of faith is assured and draws us like a
magnet, despite all.

JOHN 10.1–10

The image is not sentimental but down to earth. The shepherd values the sheep
because they are his property. What is more, he is the only true and reliable
guardian of the flock. These are Jesus' roles towards us.

- *Do we see our faith as chiefly an individual thing or a life we live with
  others?*

- *Can we identify with a positive Christian valuing of the sufferings that
  come our way?*

- *We must recognize Christ as the only true basis and measure of our value
  and our security.*

FIFTH SUNDAY OF EASTER

GENESIS 8.1–19

The day of relief and final safety for Noah is taken up in the Church as a symbol of Jesus fulfilling our dreams. So it serves well for the Easter season.

OR ACTS 7.55–60

Stephen, first martyr for Christ, dies with words on his lips that echo those of Jesus at his dying (as described in Luke 23.34, 46). The disciple is to be as his lord and master – now as then.

1 PETER 2.2–10

It is not just the work of Jesus that we must see as God's new deed in our midst, but the creation of a new people or community, taking over the inheritance and task of the Israel of old. Words that echo the Old Testament make the point.

JOHN 14.1–14

We tend always to ask for more – from God as in other, more mundane areas of life. But we should rest content. In Christ, God has amply supplied all we can truly need.

- *We are to see martyrs of any time, including our own day, as especially sharp images of genuine Christian life. Which martyrs do you find especially meaningful?*

- *To be Christian is to belong to a 'new people' that transcends other bodies we may also be members of.*

- *How hard is it truly to believe in the adequacy of God's gift to us in Christ?*

SIXTH SUNDAY OF EASTER

GENESIS 8.20—9.17

The saga of Noah has its climax in the bond God made with him, which has the rainbow as its symbol. Mutual trust and fidelity are promised. The bond is taken up for us in Jesus-centred terms.

OR ACTS 17.22–31
Paul's address in Athens seeks common religious ground with pagan Greeks, but takes care to go beyond it with the distinctive Christian message as his punchline. It makes a strategy to think about.

1 PETER 3.13–22

These words are written for Christians facing dire attack. But their sense of great crisis speaks in its way to lesser crises too and sharpens up our duller reactions.

JOHN 14.15–21

The constant presence of Christ is assured, a presence of love which carries the necessity of obedience to his overriding command – that we love one another.

- *It is important to know and value both what we share with other seekers for truth and what our own Christian contribution is. No good comes from either despising the first or underplaying the second.*

- *Pray for grace not to lose touch with the greatness of Christ's suffering for us.*

- *Is it hard to believe that love is the only bond that finally counts in the life of those who serve God?*

ASCENSION DAY

DANIEL 7.9–14

This fantastic picture certainly takes us to another realm and helps to make the point of Jesus' heavenly role in glory.

OR ACTS 1.1–11
This act, assuring Jesus' triumph, marks the transition to the time of the Church.

EPHESIANS 1.15–23

The writer sings a hymn of adoration for Christ in the heavenly endorsement of his triumph.

LUKE 24.44–53

Luke's Gospel ends with Jesus' heavenly withdrawal at the end of Easter Day – and the disciples go to the Temple, keeping the link with Israel.

- *Pray to identify with Christ as joining earth and heaven.*
- *We praise God for his gifts in Christ.*
- *Can we bear too strong a sense of glory?*

SEVENTH SUNDAY OF EASTER

(SUNDAY AFTER ASCENSION DAY)

EZEKIEL 36.24–28

The theme is restoration and homecoming, one that recurs in the Old Testament. Here, it centres on the Land of Israel – a foretaste of heaven.

OR ACTS 1.6–14

The story of the Ascension can easily seem just 'strange'. See it as a picture of the divine vindication of Jesus, leading immediately to the shared life of his followers, the infant Church.

1 PETER 4.12–14; 5.6–11

The testing of faith by persecution or otherwise is always hard; but it carries with it the seal of God's restoration and even the experience of joy.

JOHN 17.1–11

We read here the most profound of all statements about the interweaving of Jesus with the Father and then of us with them; it is our assurance for now and always.

- *Pray that the Church may always look to Jesus before it looks to itself.*

- *Can we accept the testing of our faith as in the end a benefit?*

- *The goal we share is our being involved with Christ in the life of God.*

DAY OF PENTECOST

ACTS 2.1–21

The Spirit means God as powerfully involved among us – and the story gives us
a striking picture of such power that it has made its mark on the Christian
imagination, especially in its promise of life for everyone.

OR NUMBERS 11.24–30
If only God's people shared and showed his gifts to the full. It is the dream of a
time and place when God's gifts visibly abound.

1 CORINTHIANS 12.3B–13

The Christian community is a single whole, imbued with the single power of
God. But the roles that God inspires and enables are many and utterly varied.

JOHN 20.19–23

Jesus gives the Spirit of wholesome peace and with it the removal of sin –
which spoils his gift.

OR JOHN 7.37–39
The prophets foresaw a time when water would flow from Jerusalem to revive
the energies of all the people. Jesus is such a source, as he told the woman in
John 4 and as the cross will demonstrate, with baptism to fulfil.

- *Pray to recognize the splendour of the diverse gifts of God.*

- *Give thanks for the wonder of creation.*

- *May we recognize the gifts of the Spirit around and within us.*

TRINITY SUNDAY

GENESIS 1.1—2.4A

The writer shows the whole of creation as resulting from God's orderly purpose – no accident, no meaningless process, but rational.

OR ISAIAH 40.12–17, 27–31
The prophet praises God's creative order, now in a spirit filled with wonder – and with hope for the perfection of God's purposes for the world.

2 CORINTHIANS 13.11–13

Paul ends his letter with a farewell greeting of peace, and Christians have taken it into general use in our prayers. It tells of God's all-embracing gift of himself to us.

MATTHEW 28.16–20

Jesus left behind a legacy of teaching and a mission for us to fulfil – for the good of all humankind.

- *Pray for the wholesome peace which God offers us.*
- *Praise God for the glory of creation.*
- *Pray for our part in making the gospel known.*

CORPUS CHRISTI/THANKSGIVING FOR HOLY COMMUNION

GENESIS 14.18–20

A mysterious story of Abraham meeting Melchizedek. Christians seized on the reference to bread and came to treat the story as a foretaste of the Eucharist.

1 CORINTHIANS 11.23–26

The story of the Last Supper as remembered by Paul and told chiefly to recall the Corinthian Christians to its meaning and its solemnity.

JOHN 6.51–58

Jesus gives no less than his whole self to his people – in life, in death, and in bread and wine.

- *We praise God for the constant gift of the Holy Eucharist.*
- *How thankful we must be for the visible sign of God's generosity to us.*
- *Pray never to spoil the clarity and simplicity of the gift.*

PROPER 3

(SUNDAY BETWEEN 22 AND 28 MAY INCLUSIVE, IF AFTER TRINITY SUNDAY)

ISAIAH 49.8–16A

In a passage of beautiful poetry, the prophet has in view a time when God will fill his people, at last, with fulfilment and delight.

1 CORINTHIANS 4.1–5

Paul claims only one distinction: as 'steward' of God's 'mysteries'. His apostolic role is all, and on that he is content to be judged.

MATTHEW 6.24–34

Jesus calls for a profound hatred of anxiety. God is to be trusted – whatever the appearances. And the Kingdom of God is our only concern.

- *Can we truly lay our fretfulness safely at God's door?*
- *Pray for the gift of contentment with our role in God's purpose.*
- *May we learn to trust in the provision of God.*

PROPER 4

GENESIS 6.9–22; 8.14–19

The story of the making and entering of the ark speaks of Providence for those chosen by God.

OR DEUTERONOMY 11.18–21, 26–28

Here at least, Israel's religion seems relentless and unyielding. It centred more on a way of life than a scheme of belief, and demanded observance above all. A stark choice is presented – to obey or to evade. Does that now seem the whole story?

ROMANS 1.16–17; 3.22B–28 (29–31)

Paul insists that God accepts us, not because of any merits we may or may not possess, but freely of his own sheer grace – at the cost of Christ's life given for us.

MATTHEW 7.21–29

These last words of the Sermon on the Mount redress the balance yet again. They seem to strike a note of caution by comparison with Paul's dramatic message. Moral obedience, relentless following of Jesus through thick and thin, is not sidelined by the drama of our response of pure faith.

- *Is it not good for us sometimes to see things as black and white? But with dangers?*

- *We thank God for the gift of faith – it is not our achievement in the least.*

- *There is a mystery in where we recognize authority, and it is often both hidden and complex. What part does Jesus play for us?*

PROPER 5

(SUNDAY BETWEEN 5 AND 11 JUNE INCLUSIVE, IF AFTER TRINITY SUNDAY)

GENESIS 12.1–9

The call of Abraham and the promise to him by God is central to Israel's self-awareness. And for Christians, it is a picture of God's endless fidelity to his own – by which we live.

OR HOSEA 5.15—6.6
The prophet saw past the ritual-centred everyday religion of Israel. Observance may be good but beyond and beneath it is love for God – the heart's gift. God meets that more than halfway.

ROMANS 4.13–25

Abraham was the 'father' of Israel – in him its life as a people was seen to have begun. Paul seeks to show that he lived, as Christians must live, by faith and not by observance of the law. Abraham can therefore be also a hero for Paul's gentile converts, and so a forerunner of us all. Paul was giving an important olive branch to unite gentile converts with ex-Jews.

MATTHEW 9.9–13, 18–26

Jesus' love and acceptance are wide and deep, welcoming the outcasts of society and overcoming death itself. This is close to the heart of his gift to us.

- *Is habit a strength or a blockage for true religion? Or is it both?*

- *Abraham matters less to us than to Paul, but the primacy of faith still cries out.*

- *We rejoice in Jesus' breaking of all society's mean and conventional boundaries.*

PROPER 6

GENESIS 18.1–15 (21.1–7)

God promises to Abraham and Sarah, who are very old indeed, the gift of a son who will be the bearer of the God-given vow to Abraham.

OR EXODUS 19.2–8A

In the course of the wilderness journeying of Israel after the Exodus from Egypt, God assures his people of their precious standing in his eyes. To be God's own is awesome – and laden with responsibility.

ROMANS 5.1–8

This is a key passage in Paul's letters, summing up his sense of Christ's unique role and achievement. He gave himself for sinful humans – and raised us up to the heights. 'Sharing God's glory', neither more nor less.

MATTHEW 9.35—10.8 (9–23)

Jesus sends his disciples out on a mission and here are his instructions. They are not orders for everyday life, but for special times and special duties where self-abandonment and simplicity are the keynotes. And our hearts are moved, however our journey goes.

- *God rescued Israel from Egypt as on an eagle's wings. Oh, if we could soar in our prayer and rest safe in God.*

- *If only we could grasp the depth of Christ's self-giving for us.*

- *Is our own 'self-abandonment' for God currently on the right lines?*

PROPER 7

GENESIS 21.8–21

It is not easy to see why this episode should figure in the lectionary, except
that Paul seized upon it for allegorical treatment in Galatians 4.21–31. He saw
it as prefiguring the emergence of the Church, over against old Judaism.

OR JEREMIAH 20.7–13

The prophet knows nothing but rejection for speaking out in God's cause, and
the pain is severe to the point of doubt; though he knows God's comfort. We
admire, but can we identify with Jeremiah?

ROMANS 6.1B–11

We often call baptism a 'rite of passage' – but for what transition? From womb
to world? Non-existence to life? Husband and wife to daddy-and-mummy-
plus-one? From outside to inside the Church? That is certainly warmer. But Paul
goes further. It is a death and resurrection – like Christ's, and in relation to him
alone. It is a sacrament of power indeed.

MATTHEW 10.24–39

Jesus presents vividly both the high cost of following him and the great reward
on offer from God; and notably the emphasis is on the infinite worth of each
of us in his eyes.

- *To be God's spokesperson can be a task only for the brave.*
- *Reflect on the depth of meaning in the baptism we have received.*
- *Pray to recognize how greatly God values you, and how special are your
  gifts.*

PROPER 8

(SUNDAY BETWEEN 26 JUNE AND 2 JULY INCLUSIVE)

GENESIS 22.1–14

The terrifying story of the near-sacrifice of Isaac has always been seen as pre-figuring the sacrifice of Jesus – for us (cf. Romans 8.32, where Paul looks back at it).

OR JEREMIAH 28.5–9
The situation described is remote from us, but the underlying point is clear enough. How do you tell whether a spokesperson for God is genuine or false? The answer given is: are the words borne out by events? Or, the proof of the pudding is in the eating! But is there more to be said?

ROMANS 6.12–23

Paul presents stark choices. We can serve 'sin' or 'righteousness', twin powers seeking our loyalty. Each has its inevitable end, 'death' or 'life'. But the former is for us to earn; the latter comes only by God's free gift. Can we bear to receive such bounty – and by such a means?

MATTHEW 10.40–42

The words end Jesus' instruction to missionaries of the gospel. They will radiate the reward of Jesus to those who receive them and help them on their way.

- *How dependent should we be on being certain?*
- *Pray to see where choices simply have to be made and kept.*
- *Give thanks for the ways the gospel has radiated to us.*

PROPER 9

(SUNDAY BETWEEN 3 AND 9 JULY INCLUSIVE)

GENESIS 24.24–38, 42–49, 58–67

The blood-line of Abraham, carrying God's promise for ever, must be preserved with infinite care and at all costs. No short-termism here.

OR ZECHARIAH 9.9–12

The passage is full of excitement at the prospect of rescue and vindication for God's people. There is a strong sense of the boundless extent of his joyful power.

ROMANS 7.15–25A

Paul describes the inner struggle we may endure before responding to God's shining gift in Christ. Perhaps we have to repeat the process again and again through our lives.

MATTHEW 11.16–19, 25–30

Jesus was not known for his ascetic strictness of life, and he opens his heart as widely as can be. It is a lesson to Christians inclined to be niggardly and narrow-minded in the name of religion. In Jesus' service we are as free as air, with all the burdens lifted – except the 'light' one of his service.

- *How often do we fail through narrowness of vision?*

- *Inner struggle can be the necessary prelude to a worthwhile outcome.*

- *Pray to trust in the freedom that life in Christ offers to us.*

PROPER 10

(SUNDAY BETWEEN 10 AND 16 JULY INCLUSIVE)

GENESIS 25.19–34

At each generation, choices must be made. Jacob is not 'nicer' than Esau, he is simply the one chosen. We can think of parallels in many areas!

OR ISAIAH 55.10–13
The prophet paints a joyful picture of God's purpose which achieves good results in all directions and all spheres. There is, in the end, no failure in God's work.

ROMANS 8.1–11

Paul has the positive sense of what Christ has achieved and there is no question of 'partly' or 'perhaps'. Flesh here means not 'body' but us, stuck in our own weakness and meanness; and 'Spirit' here means the liberating power of God, taking over our whole selves.

MATTHEW 13.1–9, 18–23

The parable is so familiar and seems so much a matter of common sense that we may miss its drive. All sorts of resistance and failure happen, but the push of the story is towards the good soil, where success is abundant.

- *How hard do we find it actually to rejoice in the good purpose of God?*
- *Does the sharp contrast of 'flesh' and 'Spirit' alarm or encourage us?*
- *Can we tell which kind of soil truly attracts us and holds us?*

PROPER 11

GENESIS 28.10-19A

Jacob's vocation is ratified by his encounter with God at Bethel ('house of God'). It is an image that has moved many Christians too (and see John 1.51).

OR WISDOM OF SOLOMON 12.13, 16-19
To be confident in life under the one and only God is to feel at ease in the pursuit of all that is good.

OR ISAIAH 44.6-8
This prophet was perhaps the first to see clearly that there really is only one God (and that the gods of the nations were an illusion). It is exciting to realize afresh, as if from scratch, what this entails for us.

ROMANS 8.12-25

Paul saw that we Christians are not like subjects of a lord or monarch but are like members of a family, marked by love and acceptance for our own sake – and by hope that all shall be well.

MATTHEW 13.24-30, 36-43

Matthew gives us a parable offering a stark and frightening choice, with a future to match. The message is that we should not relax in complacent ignorance of the choice, but buckle to in the Christian task.

- *Do we take God's amazing 'oneness' for granted?*

- *To be aware of our liberty is surely to be full of hope for all good.*

- *Evil oppresses the world but we hold fast to God's victory, with its signs all around us.*

PROPER 12

(SUNDAY BETWEEN 24 AND 30 JULY INCLUSIVE)

GENESIS 29.15–28

We read a love story which takes the account of the origins of God's people one step further.

OR 1 KINGS 3.5–12
Solomon, a hero-king of Israel, modestly asked for the gift of wisdom. Not a bad choice – but a brave one – for any up-and-coming person with a serious job to do.

ROMANS 8.26–39

The passage leads up to the most confident and triumphant cry of Christian faith in all the New Testament. No hostile force can finally count against the love of God.

MATTHEW 13.31–33, 44–52

The cause of God, whose success is assured, is so precious that we should forgo anything to grasp it for ourselves. To be on God's side is our ultimate good.

- *Pray for the gift of wise discernment in the problems that face us.*

- *We have every reason to face our adversities with courage from God.*

- *Reflect on where the rule of God comes in your scale of values.*

PROPER 13

(SUNDAY BETWEEN 31 JULY AND 6 AUGUST INCLUSIVE)

GENESIS 32.22–31

Our relationship with God is so serious that conflict and disputing with God are not ruled out. It may be a step on the journey.

OR ISAIAH 55.1–5
The invitation from God is open and generous, offered to more and more people.

ROMANS 9.1–5

Paul is embarking here on a long discussion about how Jews and gentiles share together in God's purpose and gift. He begins by recognizing the Jews' long role as first receivers of that gift – and we are reminded of it here.

MATTHEW 14.13–21

The story of the crowd being fed by Jesus must always have made Christian people think of the Eucharist – God's free and abundant gift to his people, expressed in simple bread but so full of meaning.

- *We recognize that our faith does not come from nowhere but, for each of us, has deep-laid roots that we easily forget.*
- *Thank God for his constant goodness.*
- *We thank God for the greatness of his sacramental gift to us.*

PROPER 14

(SUNDAY BETWEEN 7 AND 13 AUGUST INCLUSIVE)

GENESIS 37.1–4, 12–28

The story of the family strife that led into Joseph's being sold into Egypt – with, in due course, huge results for his people.

OR 1 KINGS 19.9–18
Elijah, desolate and demoralized, finds God in 'a sound of sheer silence' (a better but more mysterious translation than the old 'still small voice'); and it is a good launch-pad for the strong action for God that he goes on to take.

ROMANS 10.5–15

Paul finds scriptural backing for the core of his message and mission: that God's acceptance is open to all. Jews and gentiles alike can join in faith in Jesus.

MATTHEW 14.22–33

The Gospel gives us a picture of God's utter reliability in life's storms. Yet on our part, trust in God can always be strengthened, as testing may show.

- *Pray to value 'sheer silence' at the heart of spiritual life.*
- *Can we accept gladly that God has no favourites?*
- *Pray for the deepening of trust in God's love and power.*

PROPER 15

(SUNDAY BETWEEN 14 AND 20 AUGUST INCLUSIVE)

GENESIS 45.1–15

The long-delayed reconciliation between Joseph and his brothers brings Israel's sojourn in Egypt ever closer – with fateful results.

OR ISAIAH 56.1, 6–8
Some voices in the later Old Testament writings look beyond Israel to the wider world as they consider the scope of God's love. For them, it is clear that it must be universal.

ROMANS 11.1–2A, 29–32

In the light of Christ, Paul builds on the insights found in the reading from Isaiah and holds to his conviction of Christ's role for everybody.

MATTHEW 15.(10–20), 21–28

The Canaanite woman serves as a test case for Jesus' ministry of rescue for all. She perseveres and her need is met.

- *Can we stop ourselves putting limits of some kind on our sense of God's love for his creation?*

- *Pray to have a simple faith in God's concern for all.*

- *Do we need to persevere more doggedly in our faith in God and not be discouraged?*

PROPER 16

(SUNDAY BETWEEN 21 AND 27 AUGUST INCLUSIVE)

EXODUS 1.8—2.10

Israel's stay in Egypt became a time of servitude, but the birth of Moses is the hidden beginning of the people's release. Through 'death' to 'new life'.

OR ISAIAH 51.1-6

Two contrasting thoughts: first, behind our desired future lies our valuable past ('the rock from which you were hewn'), and the two must belong together; but second, the greatness of God dwarfs us all.

ROMANS 12.1-8

Christians are to be distinct from the society around – in the world but not of it. The reason is that it is Christ who gives us our shared identity and makes us one.

MATTHEW 16.13-20

To say 'Yes' to Jesus leads straight to a practical role. Peter (his name means 'rock') signifies the Church in all its day-to-day life and whose ultimate victory on behalf of God is sure.

- *It is hard to keep a balanced sense of our importance before God. Not too much, not too little.*

- *Do we see the Christian community as truly Christ's people – and that alone?*

- *Pray that confession of Christ leads us to a live part in his purpose.*

PROPER 17

EXODUS 3.1–15

Moses' encounter with God at the burning bush is crucial – a sacred moment: with the name of God, Moses receives his orders.

OR JEREMIAH 15.15–21
The service of God is not an easy ride and we can protest to him at its impossibility; but he will surely see us through.

ROMANS 12.9–21

Paul gives simple and basic moral teaching, some of it echoing Jesus in the Gospels. Much of it is not unusual – but that makes it no easier to accept and follow, except in God's grace.

MATTHEW 16.21–28

It is a solemn message. To follow Jesus is essentially to share the cross and all that it entails for our way of life. That is the unavoidable route to success and triumph.

- *To rail at God can be a form of faithfulness.*

- *Pray even to accept ill from others with true patience.*

- *Can we bear to become nothing for the sake of having everything that matters in the end?*

PROPER 18

(SUNDAY BETWEEN 4 AND 10 SEPTEMBER INCLUSIVE)

EXODUS 12.1–14

The rules for the meal of the Passover have always been crucial for the Jewish people. They tell of the great release, to which the meal was the prelude, and for us give promise of Jesus' act of redemption.

OR EZEKIEL 33.7–11
The prophet is God's watchman, bringing due warning to his people when their faithfulness falters.

ROMANS 13.8–14

Paul's moral teaching echoes Jesus' own stress on the command to love – and we live the good life always in the setting of the urgency of Christ's call.

MATTHEW 18.15–20

Matthew provides a stern process for the discipline of the Christian community, but promises his own good presence to his people when they meet.

- *Pray to commemorate past blessings with joy.*
- *May we heed the wise teaching that we hear.*
- *Thank God for the good fellowship we enjoy.*

PROPER 19

(SUNDAY BETWEEN 11 AND 17 SEPTEMBER INCLUSIVE)

EXODUS 14.19–31

The fearsome story of the Israelites' escape may now make us conscious of the Egyptians' horrific fate.

OR EXODUS 15.1B–11, 21B
It may now seem wicked to rejoice in our own success at the expense of gruesome horrors for others.

OR GENESIS 50.15–21
The life of God's people seems to hang by a thread, and it takes Joseph's gracious act for things to be carried forward.

ROMANS 14.1–12

Christians, like others, can squabble and divide about matters that seem to be, in the end, of minor importance. Only love can restore a true sense of proportion.

MATTHEW 18.21–35

This is a terrifying parable bringing home dramatically the message of the Lord's Prayer – to forgive readily, as we ourselves are forgiven by God.

- *How hard it is to trust that, even despite all appearances, all shall be well.*
- *Pray always to hold to the great signs of God's love.*
- *Pray to be forgiving to others, for we also are forgiven much.*

PROPER 20

(SUNDAY BETWEEN 18 AND 24 SEPTEMBER INCLUSIVE)

EXODUS 16.2–15

God's people grumble their way through the wilderness, and God's care is firm but tangible. Discipline is the dominant note.

OR JONAH 3.10—4.11

The book of Jonah is a short story about repentance and God's forbearance, even to foreigners, outside the people of Israel – and the 'righteous' do not always like God for it.

PHILIPPIANS 1.21–30

Paul wants to encourage his converts at Philippi and shows himself a good and wise pastor, who has suffered as they do – and has stood firm.

MATTHEW 20.1–16

No parable of Jesus strikes us as more shocking than this. What sort of world is it about? It is not about our world, but God's – where, fortunately for us, his grace takes no account of our deserts.

- *Do we resent God's goodness, extending even to our enemies?*

- *Christian ministry is family-like – given to us, but from alongside us.*

- *Pray to be glad that God has no favourites.*

PROPER 21

(SUNDAY BETWEEN 25 SEPTEMBER AND 1 OCTOBER INCLUSIVE)

EXODUS 17.1–7

Grumbling from below meets, as always, provision from above. Not a pleasing picture, but not beyond our experience.

OR EZEKIEL 18.1–4, 25–32

It is easy to blame some of our ills and sins on forces outside ourselves – upbringing, the culture, our society, the way the world is. Whatever the truth of that, God takes us for what we are – responsible individuals, all of us having the potential for glory.

PHILIPPIANS 2.1–13

The drama of Christ's self-humbling and his vindication by God is at the heart of our faith. It gives us the best clue we have to the mystery of our own life and destiny.

MATTHEW 21.23–32

If people cannot see Jesus' meaning from his conduct in his ministry, the fault is their own. Those pleased with their own goodness are the last people to grasp the character of God.

- *Pray to discriminate between what life virtually forces us to be and what we let ourselves become.*

- *The gift of humility is surely a matter of being 'real' before God and everyone else.*

- *We wish to be delivered from stubborn blindness to Truth when it stares us in the face.*

PROPER 22

(SUNDAY BETWEEN 2 AND 8 OCTOBER INCLUSIVE)

EXODUS 20.1–4, 7–9, 12–20

The Ten Commandments retain a place in Christian teaching, but they began with old Israelite circumstances in mind – and Jesus gave a new slant to ethics with the stress on love.

OR ISAIAH 5.1–7
The prophet's poem tells of God's patient fidelity to his people – and his endless love.

PHILIPPIANS 3.4B–14

Paul breaks out in a fusion of his pride in his Jewish credentials with the utter priority of confidence in his Christian apostolic calling – until the end.

MATTHEW 21.33–46

The parable tells of the long and varied flaws and failures of Israel as God's people. No wonder God has made a new start.

- *Pray to rejoice in God's guidance to us all.*
- *We praise God for his constancy.*
- *May we resist all complacency in our relationship with God.*

PROPER 23

(SUNDAY BETWEEN 9 AND 15 OCTOBER INCLUSIVE)

EXODUS 32.1–14

The crisis of the making of the golden calf has become an emblem of all kinds of idolatry and foolish veneration. Its message stands.

OR ISAIAH 25.1–9
It is often harder for us than for our ancestors to receive God with such ecstatic joy, even when we recognize his love towards us and the promise of fulfilment he offers to us.

PHILIPPIANS 4.1–9

Familiar words, speaking of the positive comforts that follow from God's gift of himself to us, summed up in wholesome and full-blooded 'peace'.

MATTHEW 22.1–14

In origin, the parable, put in brutal terms, is about the rejection of Christ by his own people and his acceptance by others – who should nevertheless not presume on their unmerited call.

- *Praise God for the joy of his open invitation to us, regardless of merit.*

- *Pray to know the peace that is beyond our capacity to grasp.*

- *God gives – but to take him for granted is to put love in danger.*

PROPER 24

(SUNDAY BETWEEN 16 AND 22 OCTOBER INCLUSIVE)

EXODUS 33.12–23

The work of a religious leader is often far from easy and may drive to despair. But God's presence will not fail in the crisis.

OR ISAIAH 45.1–7

A widening of Israel's view of God. He will use even pagan kings for his sovereign purposes. His writ knows no frontiers. It was, then, a daring idea.

1 THESSALONIANS 1.1–10

The opening of Paul's earliest letter. We can sense the fervour and novelty of the mission he had embarked upon in an alien land, far from home – for the sake of God's love for all, shown in Christ.

MATTHEW 22.15–22

If we hear aright, the message is not 'so much for the state' and 'so much for God or the Church' (how could one make such a bargain?) but 'all things are God's, and all other duties are second to him'. Jesus thumps the table as he utters those last words.

- *We would not dream of seeing God as somehow British; but do we sometimes get close to it?*

- *Pray to share the courage and width of imagination shown by Paul the apostle.*

- *Where might we let conflicts of loyalty move us?*

PROPER 25

(SUNDAY BETWEEN 23 AND 30 OCTOBER INCLUSIVE

DEUTERONOMY 34.1–12

The death of Moses on the eve of Israel's entry into the land of promise tears the heart. Parallels spring to mind, and many people have lesser versions of such a testing.

OR LEVITICUS 19.1–2, 15–18
The holiness of God must rub off on his people – and be expressed in down-to-earth morality, like the love of those around us.

1 THESSALONIANS 2.1–8

Paul bares his soul to his converts. His genuineness comes across with great force, as does his total commitment as a pastor.

MATTHEW 22.34–46

The focusing of Jesus on the two commands, to love God and to love our neighbour, is a great foundation for all moral teaching, leaving us much work to do.

- *Pray to discern how the two great commands work out for us.*

- *May we never lose our sense of the holiness of God.*

- *Thank God for experience of good pastoral care.*

BIBLE SUNDAY

NEHEMIAH 8.1-4A (5-6), 8-12

After the exile of leading Jews to Babylon in the sixth century BC, the return
over a century later was marked by a new focus on the sacred books of the
Law (which became the first five books of our Old Testament). They were
becoming the heart and symbol of Israel's life.

COLOSSIANS 3.12-17

Paul gives a serene and happy picture of the Christian common life: virtues
crowned with love and the singing of joyful songs of faith. Maybe Colossians
1.15-20 was one of them.

MATTHEW 24.30-35

Jesus foretells his return as part of the drama of the end of the present world
order – but his teaching will endure through everything that happens in the
process.

- *Consider what is the core of your identity as a Christian.*
- *Can we enter into the joyful picture of shared Christian life painted by Paul?*
- *In what spirit do we look to the future of God's world? Hope? Trust? Indifference?*

DEDICATION FESTIVAL

(FIRST SUNDAY IN OCTOBER OR
LAST SUNDAY AFTER TRINITY)

1 KINGS 8.22–30

The building of the first Temple in Jerusalem by Solomon was the founding not just of a place where God could be known but also a reminder that God cannot in fact be tied down.

OR REVELATION 21.9–14
The seer looks to a glorious end to all things when God and humans will at length be in unity in a community of peace.

HEBREWS 12.18–24

Meeting God is no light matter – whether in our privacy or in places we dedicate for the purpose. Such places speak of that which is beyond our capacity to handle.

MATTHEW 21.12–16

The so-called 'cleansing' of the Temple speaks to us of both the sacredness of the place and its limitations – God is never 'enclosed', but is free.

- *Thank God for holy places that we value.*

- *Pray – equally – to avoid the temptation to make idols of that which is less than God.*

- *We long to recognize that all places are sacred – to God and for God.*

ALL SAINTS' DAY (1 NOVEMBER) AND ALL SAINTS' SUNDAY

ISAIAH 56.3-8
OR ISAIAH 25.3-9 OR 2 ESDRAS 2.42-48 OR
WISDOM OF SOLOMON 3.1-9 OR DANIEL 7.1-3, 15-18

We read of a wonderful vista of prosperity and happiness for the people of God, in which all are welcome. It puts some of our little hopes in the shade. Wisdom expresses these things more soberly, but still confidently.

REVELATION 7.9-17
OR REVELATION 21.1-6A OR HEBREWS 12.18-24 OR
EPHESIANS 1.11-23 OR 1 JOHN 3.1-3

Revelation presents a vision of nothing less than a new creation – and God has all in his hand, from beginning to end. The Letter to the Hebrews and John's Epistle show us the wonder of accepting God's love and trusting in the vision of his truth.

MATTHEW 5.1-12
OR LUKE 6.20-31 OR JOHN 11.32-44

The Beatitudes, or 'blessings', which we trust to receive, are more 'spiritual' in Matthew, more 'down to earth' in Luke: and both dimensions are necessary for our souls' health. The raising of Lazarus is a vivid foreshadowing of the blessed life to which we are called.

- *Do we dare to enter into the vivid hopes that the Bible presents to us?*
- *We are to be encouraged by the picture of God's future and reach out to grasp it.*
- *The vision of God, which is the goal of sanctity, is an unfashionable objective. How do you feel about it?*

FOURTH SUNDAY BEFORE ADVENT

MICAH 3.5-12

The prophets of Israel could be firm in condemning slackness and corruption in society, even when it might cost them dear.

1 THESSALONIANS 2.9-13

Paul is not averse to being proud of his achievements and their cost in labour and privation. The gospel is serious business.

MATTHEW 24.1-14

Like many Jews, Jesus is shown foreseeing a time of great hardship that will precede the glorious triumph of God.

- *Pray for the gift of a social conscience.*
- *Thank God for witness to him in times good and bad.*
- *We trust to endure in faith.*

THIRD SUNDAY BEFORE ADVENT

WISDOM OF SOLOMON 6.12–16 OR 6.17–20

There is no sign of awesome crisis, as in most of the season's readings. Rather we are taught the duty of contemplation – of God's wise doctrine for the good of our lives.

OR AMOS 5.18–24

The prophet warns against complacent views of God's coming 'day'. No, it will be a day of fearsome challenge when human indulgence will meet its doom.

1 THESSALONIANS 4.13–18

Paul is assured that Christ will soon return and rescue his people, few though they may be. His perspective did not foresee the many centuries still to run.

MATTHEW 25.1–13

The message is that vigilance before God is a vital part of the Christian life. The image of the wedding reminds us of the fulfilment that the new world brings.

- *Give thanks for the ever-open invitation of God held towards us.*

- *Pray for the gift of vigilance in God's service in our daily life.*

- *May we never lose heart as we watch and pray.*

SECOND SUNDAY BEFORE ADVENT

ZEPHANIAH 1.7, 12–18

The prophet gives a vivid picture of the awesome future God has in store for a rebellious world.

1 THESSALONIANS 5.1–11

Paul is convinced that God's intervention is near – fearful for the world at large, but joyful for God's faithful ones.

MATTHEW 25.14–30

The Parable of the Talents leaves us all feeling insecure. It is not a story to encourage the least complacency.

- *Pray to be stirred into vigilance before God.*
- *We thank God for the prodding we both need and deserve.*
- *May we love God even when he threatens.*

CHRIST THE KING

EZEKIEL 34.11–16
OR DANIEL 7.9, 10, 13, 14 OR JEREMIAH 23.1–6

Israel had a picture of the ideal king as a true shepherd of his people, providing and protecting. Daniel is more visionary, with the hope of God's intervention through a human agent ('a son of man') who will intervene with solemn majesty and judgement.

EPHESIANS 1.15–23
OR REVELATION 1.4B–8 OR COLOSSIANS 1.11–20

The Old Testament hopes now centre on Jesus, who is shown as the culmination of all God's purposes. We have a picture of triumph and fulfilment.

MATTHEW 25.31–46
OR JOHN 18.33B–37 OR LUKE 23.33–43

In their different ways, all these passages speak of Jesus' rule, whether already in his ministry or in his death (where it is revealed in gracious forgiveness) or in his role, which he outlines to Pilate in terms of true 'kingship'.

- *Pray for the grace to recognize the majesty and victory of Christ.*
- *Christ 'rules' by love: can we accept such kingship?*
- *We are glad to be called to worship God, our maker and redeemer.*

HARVEST FESTIVAL

DEUTERONOMY 8.7-18
OR 26.1-11 OR 28.1-14 OR JOEL 2.21-27

These passages remind us that our survival still depends on God's good created order, and that carries with it severe and urgent moral obligations.

2 CORINTHIANS 9.6-15
OR PHILIPPIANS 4.4-9 OR 1 TIMOTHY 2.1-7 OR 1 TIMOTHY 6.6-10 OR REVELATION 14.14-18

In their different ways, these passages urge generosity with God's material gifts and to be aware of the dangers of wealth for our integrity and purity of motive.

MATTHEW 6.25-33
OR LUKE 12.16-30 OR LUKE 17.11-19 OR JOHN 6.24-35

These passages point to a variety of lessons appropriate to the day: generosity with one's property, reliance on Christ as the God-given bread, and the duty of detachment from earthly goods.

- *How should we express our gratitude to God for the goods of this world?*
- *Can we both love and yet go beyond material gifts?*
- *Pray for real thankfulness to God.*

FIRST SUNDAY OF ADVENT

ISAIAH 64.1-9

The longing for the all-powerful and mysterious God to 'break through' to us is very deep in the religious spirit. Here it is expressed in a pure, poetic form.

1 CORINTHIANS 1.3-9

As was common in his day, Paul's letters often open, after the greeting, with thanksgiving. Here it is offered for the recent conversion to Christ of his readers, the fruit of his own mission in Corinth a short time before.

MARK 13.24-37

Here we have a longing for God, put in a Christ-centred form, but otherwise typical of its time. The imagery could not be more dramatic. But vigilance must be a key Christian quality, readiness for God's good time – is that any and every time?

- *Let attachment to God stir the heart into longing.*

- *Can we recapture the freshness of Paul's springtime of faith?*

- *Being alert for God is a quality to cultivate.*

SECOND SUNDAY OF ADVENT

ISAIAH 40.1–11

These words are taken up in the Gospels when they describe the role of John the Baptist as herald for Jesus. In origin they looked to Israel's return from captivity in Babylon in the sixth century BC; and that in turn is compared to the release from Egyptian slavery under Moses centuries before.

2 PETER 3.8–15A

This late New Testament writing seeks to preserve a sense of alert expectation when it is beginning to fade; and the best preparation for God is the living of an upright life.

MARK 1.1–8

John the Baptist, herald for Jesus, has the good role of introducing – and so beginning to explain – who Jesus is and what his role is. John lives in a manner associated with the heroic prophet Elijah, the sign of a true spokesman for God.

- *It is good to see liberation as the constant will of God.*

- *It takes effort to maintain a sense of expectancy for God – as if for a loved one.*

- *Can we too be 'introducers' or heralds for Jesus?*

THIRD SUNDAY OF ADVENT

ISAIAH 61.1–4, 8–11

In a passage used by Jesus in his Nazareth sermon (Luke 4.16ff.), the prophet paints the new world which God desires for us, with every hurt and ill done away.

1 THESSALONIANS 5.16–24

Paul makes plain the basic duties placed on the shoulders of those who await God's fulfilment.

JOHN 1.6–8, 19–28

The opening of John's Gospel is chiefly about Christ's person and significance, but the writer rather surprisingly inserts passages about John the Baptist, emphasizing his secondary yet important role. Perhaps there were followers of the Baptist who gave him a higher place and needed correcting?

- *We need ideals in order to know where to place our efforts and our hopes.*
- *Ordinary duties are not exciting but are basic to the rhythm of our lives.*
- *Jesus stands as our best and heaven-sent guide to God's character and purpose.*

FOURTH SUNDAY OF ADVENT

2 SAMUEL 7.1–11, 16

The God-given legacy of David is to be the building of the Temple in Jerusalem.

ROMANS 16.25–27

Paul's doxology ends his letter on a note of praise and thanksgiving, and it sums up Christ's role as fulfiller of God's purpose – at long last.

LUKE 1.26–28

The Annunciation story, endlessly and famously painted, is an amazing picture of the wonder of God's way of proceeding – all unexpected, calling on the 'small' of the world as the route to triumph. And Mary, humbly, accepts her role.

- *Are we happy that God's way is not 'airy-fairy' but rooted in life and events, time and place?*
- *We should feel wonder at God's gracious condescension to Mary – and to each of us in our place.*
- *The proper Christian response is grateful co-operation in what is required of us.*

CHRISTMAS DAY AND EVENING OF CHRISTMAS EVE

See Year A, page 5.

FIRST SUNDAY OF CHRISTMAS

ISAIAH 61.10—62.3

Ecstasy in the presence of God's utter generosity – that is what the prophet opens up.

GALATIANS 4.4–7

Jesus identifies with us, so that we may be one with him and be able to call God 'Father', within the divine family.

LUKE 2.15–21

Angels are heavenly, from God. Shepherds are simple folk, widely despised, on the edge of things. They meet to rejoice in Jesus' coming.

- *Let us adore God's gift of himself in Jesus, our brother.*
- *Praise God for his huge condescension.*
- *Pray to renounce all pride before the Lord.*

SECOND SUNDAY OF CHRISTMAS

See Year A, page 7.

THE EPIPHANY

ISAIAH 60.1–6

Originally an ecstatic statement of hope for the Israel of the prophet's day, Christians read these words as a foreshadowing of the happiness of the coming of Christ and his meaning for the whole world.

EPHESIANS 3.1–12

It was a major initiative when the Christian movement first stepped out of its original Jewish setting to offer its invitation to all people; the apostle Paul was the man of courage who chiefly achieved it. We are among those who owe our faith to his work.

MATTHEW 2.1–12

Full of Old Testament echoes, the story of the Wise Men moves us by its joining of splendour and simplicity, earthly repute ('Magi' were the intellectuals of the time) with timeless and divine wonder.

- *We pray to join realism about the world with boundless hope for the future under God.*

- *How hard it is – still – to embrace what is outside our own familiar circle and culture.*

- *Beneath the complexity of things, there are simple choices, simple claims to our love.*

THE BAPTISM OF CHRIST

(FIRST SUNDAY OF EPIPHANY)

GENESIS 1.1–5

In the Old Testament, water is commonly a symbol of disorder, chaos and danger. Out of it, God brings order and, ultimately, life. So the creation story opens our minds to the truth of baptism, when, through Christ, we start on the way of assured 'new creation'.

ACTS 19.1–7

Some years into the Christian mission, Paul comes across followers of the long-dead John the Baptist. Paul enables them to complete what John had begun, as they receive baptism in Jesus' name.

MARK 1.4–11

In Mark's Gospel, Jesus' baptism opens the story and strikes us with force. This act of God unites heaven and earth. Salvation is under way, and Jesus is its accredited agent. The drama has begun.

- *Can we absorb the depth of the symbolism of water, focused here on Jesus but with meaning for the whole of creation?*
- *We pray for the many for whom water is a scarce luxury. Is not baptism also a privilege to recall with gratitude?*
- *Give thanks to God for Jesus as the chosen one who brings God to us and us to God.*

SECOND SUNDAY OF EPIPHANY

1 SAMUEL 3.1–10 (11–20)

The moving story of the call of Samuel to the service of God as the great prophet in Israel is a familiar model of the mystery of God's call to us, whatever form it takes.

REVELATION 5.1–10

Revelation, set in heaven, tells us about our own lives. The picture here is one of unbearable tension. Will the scroll (and so its vital meaning) ever be opened? Will God ever make his truth known? Jesus performs the deed, and our salvation can take its course.

JOHN 1.43–51

This is John's story of the call by Jesus of early followers. He refers at the end to the story in Genesis of Jacob's ladder linking earth and heaven. Jesus is the true 'ladder' fulfilling that very role.

- *God's call takes many forms – some dramatic, some simple, but all are insistent. We need to respond to what is asked of us, willingly and faithfully.*

- *We all feel longing that we shall one day, somehow, 'understand' – the world, ourselves, God. How does what we see of Jesus help us to do that?*

- *To 'follow' Christ is to be ready for a deepening of our grasp of things and of our own role in his purpose.*

THIRD SUNDAY OF EPIPHANY

GENESIS 14.17-20

Melchizedek appears only briefly and has always been seen as a mysterious figure. Christians came to see him as one among many who foreshadow Jesus in one way or another. He brought out bread and wine. So he can be seen as a poetic sign of the Eucharist which Jesus would give as our great priest.

REVELATION 19.6-10

A wedding feast is a powerful symbol of the fulfilment we all desire and look for. Jesus and all of us who are his followers are to be assured of such consummation of our hopes and desires.

JOHN 2.1-11

This first 'sign' in the Gospel of John is a symbol of the new set-up which Jesus brings. The wine of the Gospel takes over from the water that represents Judaism – satisfactory in its way but needing radical renewal.

- *Pray for the gift of hope that our earthly acts of worship may lift us to the God of whom they speak.*

- *We are to refuse to rest content with our present sense of God and to be ready to 'see' more.*

- *Is there not always scope for our daily plod to be raised to a new level of meaning?*

FOURTH SUNDAY OF EPIPHANY

DEUTERONOMY 18.15-20

Old Israel was full of hope that God would send faithful messengers to his people, leading them in righteous paths.

REVELATION 12.1-5A

A mysterious passage about a woman bearing a child. It is one portent among many – and the meaning is far from clear.

MARK 1.21-28

Jesus' fight against all evil shows itself here in the healing of one who is mentally sick.

- *Pray to recognize genuine spokesmen and spokeswomen for God.*
- *How far should we indulge people's scruples?*
- *Pray for all in mental turmoil.*

THE PRESENTATION OF CHRIST

(2 FEBRUARY)

MALACHI 3.1-5

The final prophet in the Old Testament is poised on the brink of great new disclosure, which will both delight and terrify. There is always cost and danger in receiving what is both new and good.

HEBREWS 2.14-18

The letter to the Hebrews insists more than any other book in the New Testament on Jesus being 'one of us' – fully human and so able to fulfil his unique task of representing us before God.

LUKE 2.22-40

Luke is keen not to make too much of a divide between old Israel and the new set-up which Jesus inaugurates. So in his infancy he fulfils the old rules, and Simeon tells what is to come. For us too there is never a clean break with our past, but we take it and renew it in our growth towards God.

- *Can we incorporate disaster and crisis into our hope for what is new? Our tragedies and setbacks are the raw material of our growth.*

- *Pray to see Jesus not as remote and 'different' but as more accessible to us than we are to one another.*

- *Pray for all who assist us as we grow towards God.*

FIFTH SUNDAY OF EPIPHANY

ISAIAH 40.21–31

The wonder and marvel of God may well overwhelm us, but our joy and privilege is to rise up to meet him.

1 CORINTHIANS 9.16–23

Paul is not 'in it for the money' – and he will do anything to bring the gospel to as many as he possibly can.

MARK 1.29–39

The mission of Jesus moves between healings and other good works – and withdrawal to the stable presence of God.

- *Pray to hold fast to our Christian calling.*
- *We thank God for the gift of prayer.*
- *Adoration of God comes first in our being with God.*

SIXTH SUNDAY OF EPIPHANY

2 KINGS 5.1-14

It is a favourite spectator sport to see important people put in their place, even humiliated. But it does none of us any harm to be humbled from time to time, provided it makes us get real with God.

1 CORINTHIANS 9.24-27

In our inner lives, as in our physical selves, discipline – about prayer and service – is a necessity for our health.

MARK 1.40-45

Socially undesirable ills and features are the hardest to accept. Jesus knocks away such taboos – we should do the same.

- *Pray for the grace of humility.*
- *May we resolve to grow in self-discipline in faith.*
- *Pray for the inclusive acceptance of those around us.*

SEVENTH SUNDAY OF EPIPHANY

ISAIAH 43.18–25

God's patience with human rejection and failure is boundless. He responds always with his ever-fresh generosity.

2 CORINTHIANS 1.18–22

Paul claims that his message has never wavered. That positive truth is his only concern, and he holds fast.

MARK 2.1–12

Jesus heals as he is asked to do – but he also forgives by divine authority: and the objections to his good gifts begin.

- *Pray never to be blind to God's new gifts.*
- *May we persevere in faith.*
- *We seek healing at all levels of our lives.*

SECOND SUNDAY BEFORE LENT

PROVERBS 8.1, 22–31

In a poetic passage, God's 'wisdom' speaks as his helper in creation. The point is that the world is, despite some appearances, neither chaotic nor random. It is the fruit of God's infinite wisdom.

COLOSSIANS 1.15–20

In this passage, Jesus is seen as stepping into the shoes of 'wisdom' as depicted in a passage like that in Proverbs 8. He is the mediator of God's purposes from beginning to end, and our God comes to us 'Jesus-shaped'.

JOHN 1.1–14

John uses the image of speech ('word'), which, like wisdom, stands for God's deliberate purpose in all that he has done, always and in every way. Jesus brought this glorious purpose before our eyes, and we behold it with gladness.

- *Pray to see the world as bearing the mark of God's good purpose.*
- *Jesus makes God known to us, and through him we 'see' God.*
- *We thank God for the order of his gift and resolve not to frustrate it.*

SUNDAY NEXT BEFORE LENT

2 KINGS 2.1–12

Together with Moses, Elijah was one of the two greatest figures in the Old Testament, and the New Testament took care to show that Jesus was greater than both (see today's Gospel). Here we have the story of Elijah's 'special treatment' by God as he is carried direct to heaven, with his disciple Elisha left as his heir as God's true prophet to his people in hard times.

2 CORINTHIANS 4.3–6

Paul writes as Christ's 'apostle' or agent. In Christ, God brings to its climax the work of bringing 'light' to the world that goes back to creation itself; and light stands for all that is true, honest and good.

MARK 9.2–9

The experience of the Transfiguration is a foretaste of Jesus' high status as God's full representative for all humankind becoming plain in his death and resurrection.

- *Pray for the gift to discern true from false spokespersons on God's behalf.*
- *Pray to see below the surface – and so to recognize in Christ the full glory of God.*
- *Pray to hold on to our experience of the depth of Christ's true self.*

ASH WEDNESDAY

See Year A, page 19.

FIRST SUNDAY OF LENT

GENESIS 9.8–17

The idea of the 'covenant' between God and his people finds here its first clear example. We think of ourselves as God's servants, but he is equally bound to us, for our eternal good.

1 PETER 3.18–22

Noah and family were saved 'through water'. The writer sees this as a picture of Christian baptism, our route to salvation in face of a godless and directionless world.

MARK 1.9–15

The baptism of Jesus is not like ours. It is the giving of his unique role on God's behalf, as his agent to right all wrongs and make his rule plain, with all urgency.

- *Water threatens but also saves life. Pray to know God as our dependable rescuer.*
- *Give thanks for baptism as the route to our deepest good.*
- *Let Jesus' preaching of God's rule keep ringing in our ears.*

SECOND SUNDAY OF LENT

GENESIS 17.1–7, 15–16

God's covenant with Abraham marks out our faith as being rooted in real people who follow one another through real time, and belong together through thick and thin.

ROMANS 4.13–25

Paul saw the essence of God's relationship with Abraham to be one of faith – trust in God, come what may, with salvation as God's doing, not man's. The birth of Isaac, against all natural odds, was a picture of the death and life of Jesus who, once more against all odds, unites us to God through his dying and rising.

MARK 8.31–38

Jesus' picture of what 'following' him entails is uncompromising. There must be a real choice to enter the new world which he makes available, with its unknown risks and surrenders of life's familiar props.

- *Thank God for his constant faithfulness to his people.*
- *We rejoice to be joined to God by faith, not by any power of our own to earn his love.*
- *What does it mean for us to 'take up the cross'?*

THIRD SUNDAY OF LENT

EXODUS 20.1–17

The Ten Commandments have a venerable place in Christian life and once stood in the sanctuary of all our churches. They began as the core of the law of Israel long ago. Now, some of them are basic morality, others need interpreting and discussing to apply to modern life.

1 CORINTHIANS 1.18–25

The death of Jesus seems at first sight to be pure tragedy, and to make anything else of it seems foolish; but look again – its very weakness is the sign of God's power and wisdom.

JOHN 2.13–22

The so-called 'cleansing' of the Temple is put forward in John's Gospel as a sign pointing to Jesus' own death and resurrection, whereby he carries out fully the task of linking us to God which the old Temple aspired to achieve.

- *The Ten Commandments point to simple decency. Ought we not to aim higher than that?*

- *From Christ's weakness God's power comes before our eyes.*

- *Jesus occupies for us the central place given to the Temple in old Judaism and meets all our needs before God.*

FOURTH SUNDAY OF LENT

NUMBERS 21.4–9

A strange magical story of disease averted.

EPHESIANS 2.1–10

Our salvation is not our own doing but the pure gift of God, bestowed at great cost.

JOHN 3.14–21

Jesus, like the serpent of old, is lifted up to heal our deepest ills – by the gift of God, freely given.

- *We trust that we may be aware of our need of God.*
- *Pray to throw our whole selves on God's great love.*
- *God loves the world, his creation, destined for all good.*

MOTHERING SUNDAY

See Year A, page 24.

FIFTH SUNDAY OF LENT

(PASSIONTIDE BEGINS)

JEREMIAH 31.31–34

This was a favourite passage among early Christians, echoed for instance in the words over the wine at the Last Supper. The prophet looks to a day when God will, as if afresh, make the closest of bonds with his own. So he will fulfil our deepest longings.

HEBREWS 5.5–10

The writer seizes on a verse in Psalm 110 which looks to an eternal priest, to be in the line of Melchizedek who appeared briefly and intriguingly in Genesis 14. Jesus, he says, fulfils the role, coming out of the blue, mysteriously, to do the work that God assigned to him, even at the cost of his life. See the image as strangely poetic.

JOHN 12.20–33

Jesus here looks to his coming death and the momentous harvest of souls to which it will lead over century after century and in countless lands.

- *How can we maintain freshness in our relationship with God?*

- *Jesus is both dependable and mysterious. Never must we take him for granted.*

- *Jesus' death is his 'glory'; it shows him in all his inner divine splendour, for those with eyes to see.*

PALM SUNDAY

(LITURGY OF THE PASSION)

ISAIAH 50.4–9A

The passage depicts a servant of God who gives himself to great suffering for the cause he has embraced.

PHILIPPIANS 2.5–11

We should probably read this passage as an early Christian hymn, summing up (rather like a kind of creed) the career of Christ – from God's highest place of esteem and dignity to the degradation of death by crucifixion, and then to glorious vindication.

MARK 14.1—15.47 OR MARK 15.1–39 (40–47)

The Passion as told in Mark (our oldest account) is bleak in the extreme. It stresses Jesus' aloneness, abandoned or turned on by all. He treads the path assigned to him – for us. It is the character of God, here starkly revealed.

- *Can we bear to face the story Mark gives to us? It shames us before it brings us any peace.*
- *Is a sense of abandonment a hard but necessary condition to a sense of being loved?*
- *Jesus' 'success' or triumph is won only at the cost of extreme loss. Can we possibly enter into its reality?*

MAUNDY THURSDAY

See Year A, page 27.

GOOD FRIDAY

See Year A, page 28.

EASTER DAY

ACTS 10.34–43

After the conversion of a gentile, a Roman officer, Peter gives a succinct outline of the importance of Jesus and the gospel that flows from him. This 'witness' is the heart of the Church's mission.

OR ISAIAH 25.6–9
The prophet foretells salvation as a huge feast for God's people, and the end of all grief.

1 CORINTHIANS 15.1–11

This passage contains the earliest known summary of Christian faith, centring on the death and resurrection of Jesus. Paul gives it to testify to his own Christ-given role as 'apostle' or agent of Jesus to make the faith known.

JOHN 20.1–18

Two stories of Easter Day, telling first of the abandoned tomb and then of Jesus' meeting with Mary Magdalene. A new world is born and the old is put behind. And love and recognition are the marks of the new.

OR MARK 16.1–8
This is the oldest story of the resurrection, and we note that it gives no story of an appearance by Jesus. Indeed, it is mysterious in the extreme, with its strange ending. It is as if we are to put no trust in mere 'evidence', but to accept God's future by faith.

- *Theories are all very well, but we start from the bedrock simplicity of the Christian story and give thanks for it.*

- *We give thanks for the new life that Jesus gives and for its fruit in Paul – and in us.*

- *Pray not to fret to 'tie up' our faith but to leave room for God to show us more.*

SECOND SUNDAY OF EASTER

EXODUS 14.10–31; 15.20–21

The disaster which Passover brought to the Egyptians need give us no joy. It is chiefly a picture of miraculous rescue for freedom.

OR ACTS 4.32–35
The earliest Christian community in Jerusalem bound itself together to the point of sharing all its property. Christians have not always been happy with this generous impulse. Should they be more ready to welcome it?

1 JOHN 1.1—2.2

This letter is a pastoral statement of the precious gift of God to us in Jesus and the forgiveness that is so important a part of it.

JOHN 20.19–31

The story of Thomas reassures many who 'have not seen yet have come to believe'. Faith comes by many routes and does not depend on proof – which can indeed be its very opposite and its enemy. It is an act of self-giving love.

- *Christian common life needs to have practical expression. How far can we take it?*

- *To be a Christian is to know the renewal of life.*

- *Pray for purity of faith, for the sake of God alone.*

THIRD SUNDAY OF EASTER

ZEPHANIAH 3.14–20

The prophet sings of the liberation of God's people from captivity. It is for us a sense that we can share.

OR ACTS 3.12–19

Peter addresses a hostile audience in Jerusalem. He both excuses those who attack and who killed Jesus (they acted in ignorance) and presents them with the gospel hope. For God has vindicated Jesus, his great agent for our good.

1 JOHN 3.1–7

The promise of the vision of God himself is one of the most wonderful in the whole of the scriptures. Our destiny is no less than the closest fellowship with God that we can imagine.

LUKE 24.36–48

In this appearance, Jesus places his mission in the context of God's age-old promises and his work for his people. But a whole new time of fulfilment has now arrived.

- *We give thanks for the gift of faith given through Jesus, but we have no space for hostility to those who reject it.*

- *Pray for grace to grasp the promise of the closest intimacy with God.*

- *We thank God that always he directs his goodness towards us.*

FOURTH SUNDAY OF EASTER

GENESIS 7

The old story of the great flood and of the rescue of Noah is a familiar picture of salvation – always a miraculous and amazing gift.

OR ACTS 4.5–12

Peter uses the evidence of a healing to support his claim for Jesus as the key to salvation. Hardly enough by itself, it is a way in to making the case for Jesus. Small doors can lead into large rooms.

1 JOHN 3.16–24

The intimate relationship of Christians with Christ centres on love, his gift to us – and our readiness to share and spread it. This is the basis for our seeking after virtue. Not an individual quest but a common pursuit.

JOHN 10.11–18

The key to this easily sentimentalized picture is the sheer value of sheep to their owner. It is this that accounts for Jesus' self-offering on our behalf and for the sake of the growth of the flock. It is his God-given task.

- *Pray to seize small clues to lead us on to faith and love for God.*
- *Pray for the gift of openness to one another which is the beginning of love.*
- *Thank God for Jesus' dying as an act of sheer generosity – even for us.*

FIFTH SUNDAY OF EASTER

BARUCH 3.9–15, 32–36; 4.1–4

God's people rejoice in his favour and the wisdom that makes him known.

OR GENESIS 22.1–8

This terrifying story of disaster so narrowly averted is a picture of submission to God, even in the most extreme situation – yet also of liberation.

OR ACTS 8.26–40

This is the first instance of anyone reading the passage about the suffering servant of God in Isaiah 53 as a picture of the meaning of Jesus. It leads this foreigner (perhaps a marginal Jew) to baptism by the hand of Philip.

1 JOHN 4.7–21

'God is love.' Familiar to the point of cliché, but a major breakthrough. God might be chiefly just or even vengeful or endlessly demanding. But it is not so. Love is the key to his whole being, through and through.

JOHN 15.1–8

The image of the vine sets out a picture of the Christian community as, first, joined together totally, and, second, as wholly dependent on Christ who is himself the vine as a single entity. And then the task is to bear fruit.

- *Give thanks to God for the strange circumstances that can bring us to him.*

- *Can we accept God as totally marked by love?*

- *Pray to embrace our dependence on one another as Christian people.*

SIXTH SUNDAY OF EASTER

ISAIAH 55.1–11

The message is twofold: that God is generous and bountiful, and that he is nevertheless beyond all human imagining.

OR ACTS 10.44–48

This passage marks a decisive moment in the Church's life: when Jewish Christians were challenged to accept gentile converts for the first time. The move was made – with difficulty. Such moments of the widening of vision are always difficult – down to our own day.

1 JOHN 5.1–6

Obedience as a Christian is to be no burden because it springs from love, which comes in turn from God's love for us made plain in the offering of his life by Jesus.

JOHN 15.9–17

The Gospel of John gives us only one command to obey and it must embrace all the 'duty' that we take on: that we love one another. It sounds simple but it only becomes so if it really embraces our whole way of life.

- *Pray for courage to accept new developments where needed for the sake of the gospel.*
- *Thank God for the simplicity of obedience that underlies what sometimes seems the complexity of Christian life.*
- *Pray that we may accept ourselves as truly 'friends' of God – high status indeed.*

ASCENSION DAY

See Year A, page 35.

SEVENTH SUNDAY OF EASTER

(SUNDAY AFTER ASCENSION DAY)

EZEKIEL 36.24–28

The return of the exiles from Babylon to Judaea was a major act of salvation –
comparable to the flight from Egypt. It will produce a whole new start.

OR ACTS 1.15–17, 21–26

The story of the choice of Matthias seems at first sight just a matter of
organization. But the point is to ensure the continuity of what Jesus had set
in motion. Christians live in 'the real world', and the task is not to shun it but
to fill it with the gospel.

1 JOHN 5.9–13

This passage is a kind of summing up of leading themes of the First Letter of
John; so it is written in a set of brief headings. 'Life' is a gift of God to be
found through Jesus. Only so can we truly relate to God and each other as we
are meant to do.

JOHN 17.6–19

In this final chapter before the Passion, Jesus prays to God for those whom God
'has given him'. In so doing, he binds them in to his own union with God; and
nothing can be deeper or more thorough than that.

- *Can we pray to see behind the ordinary things of church life to the things
  of God that must fill them and give them life?*

- *Exclusiveness and superiority are not our way: pray to accept humbly
  what God gives to us.*

- *Give thanks that God has united us to himself through Jesus our Lord,
  who is God to and for us.*

DAY OF PENTECOST

ACTS 2.1–21

The Spirit means: God as powerfully involved among us – and the story gives us a striking picture of such power that it has made its mark on the Christian imagination, especially in its promise of being for everyone.

OR EZEKIEL 37.1–14
The story of the valley of dry bones to which God gives life is a fitting prophecy of the burst of new vitality and power which the earliest Church displayed.

ROMANS 8.22–27

There is always something unfinished about the gift of God, and we look for its fulfilment in a spirit of hope – a strong virtue, essential to our Christian life. It enables us to yearn for the perfection of all things in God's providence.

JOHN 15.26–27; 16.4B–15

We live in the time between the life of Jesus and the fulfilment we must hope for. We therefore have to come to terms with the conditions of this 'space'. In the light of the past, we can see the shape of the future but we cannot imagine its glory. God embraces the whole. The Spirit is the name we give to God for his work in this time between.

- *Pray for discontent with the present state of things as we look always towards God's perfecting power.*

- *Pray for the gift to rejoice in what we have received from God while embracing the Spirit that drives us forward.*

- *We trust that we may share the vigour of our first ancestors in the faith.*

TRINITY SUNDAY

ISAIAH 6.1–8

The dramatic call of the prophet Isaiah takes us to the heart of what it means to feel seized by God and to have no option but to respond and give oneself to his service. It is an act of love, a real giving of oneself, but all the same, there is a kind of glad compulsion.

ROMANS 8.12–17

For Paul, 'spirit' and 'flesh' do not quite mean soul and body but rather twin forces to which we are subject. On the one hand we can be directed towards God ('spirit') or else on the other hand towards ourselves and the ordinary horizons of this world. God can draw us to himself and then we truly know him as 'Father'.

JOHN 3.1–17

Nicodemus cannot make sense of the idea of 'rebirth'. Jesus has to explain the poetry. It is all about starting again from our foundations and entering a new sphere of life that centres on God as made known, visibly, through and in Jesus.

- *God's call can be truly dramatic as an experience, but in any case we pray for its reality in our lives.*

- *We thank God that he raises us to such a high status in his company. May we live up to it – by his grace.*

- *Pray to recall the true meaning of our baptism and to live in its light.*

CORPUS CHRISTI/THANKSGIVING FOR HOLY COMMUNION

See Year A, page 39.

PROPER 3

HOSEA 2.14–20

The prophet establishes the strong image of the bond between God and his people as like a marriage. Christians took it up for Christ and the Church.

2 CORINTHIANS 3.1B–6

Paul gives the highest praise to his converts as God's gift to him, their apostle – a role of newness and freshness which has been given to him by God.

MARK 2.13–22

The good news of the kingdom of God is all bright and fresh. Old ways and old prejudices fade from sight.

- *Pray to welcome the gospel as ever new and never fading.*
- *Thank God for the Christian community, his chosen people, united to him.*
- *We pray for the people of God, in all their varied forms.*

PROPER 4

1 SAMUEL 3.1–10 (11–20)

Samuel is the apprentice-leader of the worship of Israel, dedicated from his birth. He will soon take the place of Eli, his master, and bring a new regime for God.

OR DEUTERONOMY 5.12–15

The observance of the sabbath as 'holy day' in Israel is to remind everyone of God's rescue of his people from Egypt – it is a weekly release from toil.

2 CORINTHIANS 4.5–12

Christian leaders may be tempted to peddle their own views, even their own self-righteous pride. Not true of Paul, who gave himself through thick and thin for the cause of Christ and the gospel.

MARK 2.23—3.6

In two encounters Jesus comes up against the scruples of people who put strict obedience to the rules above every other consideration; Jesus puts human need and even cheerful common sense first.

- *Pray that concern for virtue may not blind us to human need.*

- *Thank God for Christian self-sacrifice.*

- *We praise God for the simple priorities of the gospel.*

PROPER 5

1 SAMUEL 8.4–11 (12–15), 16–20; (11.14–15)

Kings are seen in the Old Testament as a doubtful quantity: they may serve God's cause (like David, mostly), but more likely they will succumb to pride and grandeur – and subvert God's cause.

OR GENESIS 3.8–15
The story of the Fall centres on disobedience leading to the concealing of truth and then to fatal double-speak with God.

2 CORINTHIANS 4.13—5.1

For the Christian, the present state of affairs is never the last word. We reach always for the perfection that is at present beyond our grasp.

MARK 3.20–35

In this Gospel, Jesus is constantly rejected or misconstrued by those closest to him. Here, his family fail to grasp the truth that stares them in the face – so they sin against the very Spirit of God.

- *Pray never to reject wilfully the challenge of the gospel.*
- *May we be saved from complacency in our service of God.*
- *It is not for us to play games with God.*

PROPER 6

1 SAMUEL 15.34—16.13

Leadership of Israel is a succession of hopes raised then dashed, as men fail to measure up to the hopes invested in them. The Fall constantly repeats itself.

OR EZEKIEL 17.22-24

A parable of the constant failure of human conceit, as plans are thwarted and cease to flourish.

2 CORINTHIANS 5.6-10 (11-13), 14-17

Christ's effect on everything is so revolutionary that we see the whole world and our own lives with fresh eyes.

MARK 4.26-34

Jesus preaches – and 'plants' among us – the sovereignty of God; not as a mere fact but as the marvellous truth that surrounds us. This truth will spread and spread, often unseen.

- *Pray always to sense the freshness of God.*
- *Thank God for his reliability always.*
- *Pray for the growing spread of God's word.*

PROPER 7

(SUNDAY BETWEEN 19 AND 25 JUNE INCLUSIVE, IF AFTER TRINITY SUNDAY)

1 SAMUEL 17.(1A, 4–11, 19–23), 32–49

The long story of the victory of the youth David over the veteran champion, Goliath, is a literary classic. Pious lessons may seem rather forced.

OR 1 SAMUEL 17.57—18.5, 10–16

David is the returned hero, darling of the people – and a threat to those in power.

OR JOB 38.1–11

The long poem, chiefly a discussion between God and Job about the terrible ills he has suffered, ends in God crushing him. Who is Job to have an opinion? Not a satisfactory modern answer, but we can think out whether there is a point in it!

2 CORINTHIANS 6.1–13

Paul has suffered much misunderstanding in his work as apostle, even from those to whom he has been the bringer of the gospel and who owe him so much. He feels the pain but tells them of his own God-given resources. His love is not stifled.

MARK 4.35–41

The story of the calming of the storm by Jesus must have been heard by its first hearers as a picture of the truth that they were to trust, purely and simply, through all sufferings and torments that might come to them. Jesus is greater than all such ills.

- *Pray never to turn away from the sheer wonder and greatness of God.*

- *To stand for the gospel is to take risks. Pray not to shirk them out of fear.*

- *Give thanks for the calm that can lie beneath our sufferings.*

PROPER 8

2 SAMUEL 1.1, 17–27

In this classic passage, we read of David's heroic lament for Saul and
Jonathan – whose mantle he will now soon take on, though not without strife.
It is the stuff of the sagas of many nations.

OR WISDOM OF SOLOMON 1.13–15; 2.23–24

This positive statement of our essential goodness and value as God's own
handiwork should encourage us. This underlies all that goes wrong with us or
spoils us for God. To realize this is to be on the way to recovery.

2 CORINTHIANS 8.7–15

It may not be immediately obvious, but Paul is here urging his converts in
Corinth to give generously to the needs of the mother church in Jerusalem.
Perhaps they could not quite see the point. He bases his appeal on the infinite
generosity of Christ in his self-giving, working out his life and death in the
conditions of this world. They must love their fellow-Christians wherever they
are. God's people are a single family.

MARK 5.21–43

The raising of Jairus' daughter is a kind of foreshadowing of Jesus' own
resurrection, and must have been heard as such from the start. As always,
Jesus responds to human need, even in this extremity. And new life is the
outcome.

- *Give thanks for our standing as God's creatures, which is our chief glory.*

- *How can theory and practice meet in our practical generosity?*

- *Receive Jesus as the bountiful source of all kinds of good, even life itself.*

PROPER 9

(SUNDAY BETWEEN 3 AND 9 JULY INCLUSIVE)

2 SAMUEL 5.1–5, 9–10

David at length receives the throne of Israel – by popular acclaim.

OR EZEKIEL 2.1–5

The call of Ezekiel is unconditional. He simply has to obey. And that applies whether he succeeds in his mission or whether he is ignored. The necessity is simply to speak, to bear witness to the cause of God.

2 CORINTHIANS 12.2–10

Paul has been provoked by the mistrust of his converts almost to a frenzy of despair at their meanness of spirit. He reveals his deep identification with Christ. Despite the temptation to boast of his spiritual experiences (which he does not quite resist!), his real boast is in the grace of God which swamps his self-mistrust and overcomes his weakness.

MARK 6.1–13

Two themes. Jesus is received least where he is best known – at home. It rings true, yet it is not to the credit of those concerned. Is it a common feature, not to recognize the good that is under our very nose? Then: Jesus sends out his first followers to extend his own work, whatever the obstacles, in simplicity and trust.

- *Can we bear to see that sometimes devotion to God is a matter of take it or leave it?*

- *Pray to recognize when meekness has gone too far and there is need to speak.*

- *May we be protected from failure to see God's truth, even when it stares us in the face.*

PROPER 10

2 SAMUEL 6.1–5, 12B–19

The holy city now enters the story of David. The future of his dynasty begins to take fuller shape. It is laden with destiny.

OR AMOS 7.7–15
The prophet Amos was a strange and unwelcome figure, a troublemaker with his message of doom, but he was convinced that his words were what God required his people to hear. Such people are a scourge to our complacency.

EPHESIANS 1.3–14

This passage (a single sentence in Greek!) is a highly poetic piece about Christ's high role in God's purpose, from the beginning of everything to its final consummation, still to be revealed. This paean of praise brings us fully into its scope, for we are the beneficiaries.

MARK 6.14–29

The grim story of John the Baptist's martyrdom stands in its own right but is also, in the context of the Gospel as a whole, a foretaste of Jesus' own Passion which is still to come. Both fall victim to authorities that cannot bear their goodness and truth.

- *Pray for readiness to accept God's word even when it disturbs and shakes us.*
- *Praise God for the whole sweep of his great work through Christ for us.*
- *We thank God for the stirring witness of martyrs for truth and for God's cause.*

PROPER 11

(SUNDAY BETWEEN 17 AND 23 JULY INCLUSIVE)

2 SAMUEL 7.1–14A

Yet another false start, kingship in Israel is never straightforward – full of hazards and temptations, and hesitations in God's support.

OR JEREMIAH 23.1–6

As ever, the prophet stands out from the comfortable preaching of more common-or-garden spiritual leaders, and here offers a message of hope. God will restore his apparently abandoned people in the name of his righteous purpose.

EPHESIANS 2.11–22

The writer rejoices that Paul's brave and crucial mission to bring gentiles into the Christian movement alongside the original Jewish members has been a triumphant success. It is what Christ stood for, God's love for all, and is the richest kind of peace.

MARK 6.30–34, 53–56

Here we have a general passage about two sides of Jesus' work: withdrawal to recuperate for the purpose of God, and then the work itself of healing and restoration for those in need.

- *We give thanks for God's gift of hope.*

- *Praise God for the universal scope of the gospel as it has come to us.*

- *Pray to accept both the reflective and the active sides of the Christian life.*

PROPER 12

(SUNDAY BETWEEN 24 AND 30 JULY INCLUSIVE)

2 SAMUEL 11.1–15

David falls deeply into sin as his desire for Bathsheba leads him to plot murder. So the king is no flawless hero – not in the least.

OR 2 KINGS 4.42–44

This miracle of Elisha's is one of a number of his great deeds as a prophet, and it stands here as a pointer to Jesus' own feeding of the multitude in the Gospel reading. Material abundance points to the richness of God's spiritual provision.

EPHESIANS 3.14–21

We hear a great statement of praise to God for the known gift of his love to us and the boundless scale of his grace. We have the capacity to achieve far more than we care or dare to recognize.

JOHN 6.1–21

The feeding of the multitude stands in the Gospel of John as a sign which Jesus then expounds in terms of himself as the true bread from heaven. It is seen not just as a wonderful happening but as a symbol of all that he stands for in terms of God's saving generosity to us.

- *We pray that we may be 'fed' at all levels of the life that we have from God.*
- *Praise God for the scale of his gifts, so easily underestimated.*
- *May we open ourselves with imagination to God's love.*

PROPER 13

(SUNDAY BETWEEN 31 JULY AND 6 AUGUST INCLUSIVE)

2 SAMUEL 11.26—12.13A

David meets his nemesis – through Nathan, spokesman for God; and he has the grace to repent. Kings are no absolute monarchs in God's eyes.

OR EXODUS 16.2–4, 9–15

The provision of manna to the people of Israel in the wilderness is a saving gift of God – which was a model for the Christian Eucharist.

EPHESIANS 4.1–16

The writer of Ephesians moves from doctrine to exhortation, and on to conduct in the light of the doctrine. The aim is always maturity in Christ, and true unity.

JOHN 6.24–35

Picking up the image of the manna, Jesus presents himself as the 'bread of life', God's full provision for his people for ever.

- *Whether our faults are small or spectacular, repentance is an open door.*
- *Jesus himself is the full provision for our souls' need.*
- *Let us rejoice in the promise of maturity in Christ.*

PROPER 14

(SUNDAY BETWEEN 7 AND 13 AUGUST INCLUSIVE)

2 SAMUEL 18.5–9, 15, 31–33

David suffers disastrous misfortune, close as possible to his heart – it is the stuff of classic tragedy.

OR 1 KINGS 19.4–8

A simple story from the life of Elijah, illustrating his plain reliance on God's provision for his life. We note that the prophet's purpose was to be in God's special presence at Mount Horeb, a kind of equivalent to Sinai of old.

EPHESIANS 4.25—5.2

Towards the end of his letters, Paul turns to moral instruction, and here it is – simple and straightforward. The heart of all Christian morality is the need to love, just because we are ourselves already loved by Christ who 'gave himself up for us'.

JOHN 6.35, 41–51

The emphasis here falls on the solid permanence of God's gift of himself to us in Christ. This is no temporary emergency aid like the manna, but something that is 'for ever'. It belongs, that is, to a whole different dimension of things, which we refer to as 'eternity'.

- *There is room to recognize with gratitude God's simple gifts, though they are always for a great and good purpose.*

- *Pray not to neglect the simple duties which are basic to human life.*

- *Thank God for our access to the new 'world' that means the life of God.*

PROPER 15

(SUNDAY BETWEEN 14 AND 20 AUGUST INCLUSIVE)

1 KINGS 2.10–12; 3.3–14

As Solomon succeeds to David's throne, God promises even greater wealth and prestige – but always with moral proviso.

OR PROVERBS 9.1–6

This nice little picture speaks of the attractiveness we should feel for God's gift of 'wisdom', which means the intelligent appreciation of the world. It is one of God's often unrecognized gifts, and bids us go beyond emotion or solid moral conduct in our faith to the use of our brains.

EPHESIANS 5.15–20

This is one of the earliest references to Christian music: even then they had hymns to lift the soul, and it is worth reflecting on this gift of music that we so easily take for granted in the good provision for our lives, including our religious lives before God.

JOHN 6.51–58

The very solid and direct language here about the Eucharist often causes offence. It is partly designed to make us see the physical realism that is part of what we call our spiritual lives. We need such material links with God because we are people of flesh and blood who live in the world of stuff and of sense. But the subject throughout is Jesus himself.

- *Give thanks for the intelligence which we can bring to our love for God.*

- *We give thanks for the gift of music, raising us to good.*

- *Pray for readiness to bring our whole selves, body and soul, to our service of God.*

PROPER 16

(SUNDAY BETWEEN 21 AND 27 AUGUST INCLUSIVE)

1 KINGS 8.(1, 6, 10–11), 22–30, 41–43

Solomon builds the first 'house' for God, the Temple in Jerusalem. It is the solid focus of God's presence with his people, also symbolized in the ancient ark or sacred chest.

OR JOSHUA 24.1–2A, 14–18
Solemn incidents like this one serve to renew the 'covenant' or bond made between God and his people repeatedly, from Abraham on to Moses at Sinai. It puts us in mind of the 'new covenant' which Christians see firmly made in the cross of Christ.

EPHESIANS 6.10–20

This is one of the most military passages in the New Testament and has inspired warlike manifestations of our faith. But the enemy in view is forces of evil that threaten God's cause of love and find a place in all of us. The 'fight' is sustained by close attachment to God in vigilant prayer.

JOHN 6.56–69

Rounding off a series of readings from this long chapter of the Gospel of John, we find that the blunt teaching about the intimacy of Christ's self-giving to his own and his union with them leads people to hesitate and even withdraw. Jesus has always been a figure of controversy, for good reasons and bad. Faith is not without cost.

- *Thank God for his reaching out to us in the firmest of bonds.*

- *Pray for grace to recognize and combat that which is hostile to God.*

- *Our task is to remain faithful to God's truth whatever may tempt us away.*

PROPER 17

(SUNDAY BETWEEN 28 AUGUST AND 3 SEPTEMBER INCLUSIVE)

SONG OF SOLOMON 2.8–13

The love poems that make up this short book, now often neglected, give a beautiful picture which may lift our relationship with God, as individuals, to a new plane. Can we dare to find it attractive?

OR DEUTERONOMY 4.1–2, 6–9
The gift of the land to Israel was the bedrock of her faith; and it carried with it obedience to God's commands, as Deuteronomy proceeds to expound.
The passage exhorts us to hold on firmly to what we have been given, now seen by Christians in their own fresh terms; but the principle remains valid.

JAMES 1.17–27

The Letter of James is mostly taken up with simple moral teaching and is easily felt to be rather unexciting. It tells us what we already know. But we can bear the repetition from time to time – lest we forget. Simple duties conscientiously performed can be the test of faith's reality.

MARK 7.1–8, 14–15, 21–23

A selection of verses which omits some rather technical bits between the three passages given. The discussion springs from the Jewish emphasis on ritual purity, secured by ritual washings. Jesus takes our eyes away from such ceremonies and goes deeper – to the intentions of the heart and their outcome in moral acts.

- *Pray always to be aware of the sheer generosity of God to his people.*

- *We should not despise the small but often important duties that come our way.*

- *Pray to be alert to the purity of the motives that lie behind our outward deeds.*

PROPER 18

(SUNDAY BETWEEN 4 AND 10 SEPTEMBER INCLUSIVE)

PROVERBS 22.1-2, 8-9, 22-23

The writer of this book is a man of solid worth who reflects on the moral life with much decency of heart and simple but perceptive good sense. Not, however, much drama or complexity.

OR ISAIAH 35.4-7A

The passage gives a wonderful vision of the restoration of lives that God intends for us and which is at the heart of his purpose. The followers of Jesus saw these striking words fulfilled in his generous ministry of healing. It was no less than the bringing of salvation.

JAMES 2.1-10 (11-13), 14-17

The early churches (like Jesus) were no friends of the well heeled. Here, if we read carefully, we see that the very poor were also not prominent within the fellowship. As now, most Christians were of the middling sort. But the moral still has its strength, does it not?

MARK 7.24-37

The second part of the passage takes up in the healing act of Jesus precisely the words of Isaiah in today's Old Testament reading in its Greek version. The first story makes another point. Jesus is ready to countenance something quite daring in the context: bringing foreigners within the scope of his work. By the time Mark wrote, Paul had made this a glorious reality on a grand scale.

- *Pray never to lose the vision of a world restored and human life made whole.*

- *We must be on guard against complacency about wealth and property. They are given to us in trust.*

- *We trust to be free of narrowness in our sense of who is 'entitled to' the gospel.*

PROPER 19

(SUNDAY BETWEEN 11 AND 17 SEPTEMBER INCLUSIVE)

PROVERBS 1.20–33

'Wisdom' is from God: to be wise means to be open to his teaching – and being 'simple' is not a convincing excuse.

OR ISAIAH 50.4–9A

This is one of the celebrated passages in Isaiah which are easily read as foreshadowing the Passion of Jesus and are commonly read in Holy Week. It speaks of a servant of God who sees that his calling involves the enduring of suffering and persecution for God's cause. So it has always been.

JAMES 3.1–12

This warning about the dangers that beset those who reckon to pass on the faith is alarming. But it is plain truth for us all that the gift of speech carries risks as well as delights. James lays his message on in spades.

MARK 8.27–38

The message that comes first via Peter's bold but unconsidered confession is stern: to follow Jesus is to take up the cross. Mark's teaching is without light and shade. And Peter was to illustrate the point only too clearly when he denied his following of Jesus in the moment of trial.

- *There is always a risky side to taking on the cause of God. Pray to accept it.*

- *Many of us need to be more aware of the possibilities of speech – for good and ill.*

- *Following Jesus is, in essence, infinitely demanding and no picnic.*

PROPER 20

PROVERBS 31.10–31

A lone scriptural passage in praise of good wives and managers of the household. Details would now change, but we can get the message.

OR WISDOM OF SOLOMON 1.16—2.1, 12–22
Wicked people can sometimes be corrupted to their very roots and implacable in their hatred of good people. There is a sad realism here.

OR JEREMIAH 11.18–20
A briefer passage making much the same point, but also expressing a hope for retribution which the teaching of Jesus forbids.

JAMES 3.13—4.3, 7–8A

Worldly ambition easily leads us to distort truth in our own interests. The passage urges peacefulness and contentment in the pursuit of goodness and truth.

MARK 9.30–37

The disciples of Jesus are here shown, as commonly by Mark, as contentious and ambitious. They serve as a warning quite as much as an example. It is necessary to accept the role of a servant in simplicity and grace, as Jesus himself did, above all in his dying.

- *A virtuous life is no passport to a peaceful life. Can we be ready for such an outcome?*
- *Pray for the gift of single-mindedness in our goals in life.*
- *Thank God for the simplicity that the Christian faith can form within us.*

PROPER 21

ESTHER 7.1–6, 9–10; 9.20–22

Esther, Jewish captive at the Persian court, pleads for the life of her people who are under threat. She wins her request and relief is granted. A story of salvation.

OR NUMBERS 11.4–6, 10–16, 24–29

An episode from Israel's wandering in the wilderness. As usual, there is discontent and rebellion. Here God responded by a dramatic bestowal of spiritual power (and a profusion of quails follows).

JAMES 5.13–20

This passage serves as an early church model for the pastoral care of the Church's sick – and prayer books echo it. There is to be, above all, confession of sin, and prayer with anointing.

MARK 9.38–50

What to do about supporters who are not quite 'one of us'? Welcome them gladly! But corruption is another matter.

- *Pray to avoid narrowness of sympathy in the Church.*
- *When we are sick, how can we profit from full-blooded ministry?*
- *Pray for all those who care for the sick.*

PROPER 22

(SUNDAY BETWEEN 2 AND 8 OCTOBER INCLUSIVE)

JOB 1.1; 2.1–10

Job is the victim of a heavenly gamble about his fidelity to God. At huge cost his trust in God holds firm. His vindication, however, lies many pages ahead.

OR GENESIS 2.18–24

We receive the basic text that gives God's blessing to the basic naturalness of marriage. Its purpose, as seen here, is simply to provide company in a lonely world. We are only truly ourselves in interaction with others, especially those closest to us, among whom we can both give and receive.

HEBREWS 1.1–4; 2.5–12

This passage states a high doctrine of Jesus. He has put his stamp on the whole of God's creation and is now exalted to highest heaven. Yet he did come, wonderfully, 'for a little while', to be lower than the angels, then to receive highest honour. It is a dramatic picture, expounding verses of Psalm 8.

MARK 10.2–16

The Genesis passage helps us to see why Jesus, looking to human fundamentals, sees divorce as a tragedy that should not occur. It casts us back into isolation which may do us no good. There is a simplicity that is the best route to the Kingdom of God.

- *We give thanks for the underlying simplicity and wholesomeness of our basic relationships.*

- *For the eye of faith, Jesus is all embracing in his significance, and we give praise.*

- *We pray for the strengthening of the institution of marriage.*

PROPER 23

(SUNDAY BETWEEN 9 AND 15 OCTOBER INCLUSIVE)

JOB 23.1–9, 16–17

Who thinks the Bible is full of unreal piety? Job expresses a spiritual devastation, with God far away, which many can echo at times. If only all loss of faith were so hard fought!

OR AMOS 5.6–7, 10–15

The prophet Amos was one of the first we know of to attack the evils of society itself, a forerunner of many, down to our own day. He stands against the complacency which leads so many to accept social evils so long as they are profitable. Down to our own day.

HEBREWS 4.12–16

Jesus is called 'high priest', and this writing works out the image in detail later. The role in mind is that of mediator. The priest stands 'between' humans and God, making due offerings on their behalf, for the sake of their good.

MARK 10.17–31

First, Jesus goes behind even the Ten Commandments to the command to love which now has absolute priority (and so he stops the mouths of noisy moralists). Then he attacks the rich. There is no doubt that wealth is a great comfort, but it is easily a distraction from the things of God – and in the world brought by Jesus values are quite different.

- *Pray to be alert to the demands of the society in which we live.*
- *We may long for guidance, but the demand that we 'love' may be all we truly need.*
- *In what ways can we relax the hold of possessions upon our hearts?*

PROPER 24

(SUNDAY BETWEEN 16 AND 22 OCTOBER INCLUSIVE)

JOB 38.1–7 (34–41)

Not all now find God's answer to Job's problem of his unmerited suffering satisfactory. It is simply an assertion of God's power and greatness: who are we to answer back? How 'rational' can we 'reasonably' be?

OR ISAIAH 53.4–12

This chapter of Isaiah, whose original reference is obscure, is now often known as the Song of the Suffering Servant of God. All through Christian history it has been read as throwing light on what happened to Jesus and helping us to reflect on his self-giving, mysteriously, for the good of all, in the name of our holy and generous God.

HEBREWS 5.1–10

The writer picked up on Psalm 110.4, which refers to the obscure priest king of Jerusalem who comes in a story in Genesis 14. He sees him as a symbol of Jesus. The high priest of old was a mediator between his people and God, humbly offering prayer and sacrifice; in the case of Jesus his own self, body and soul.

MARK 10.35–45

Jesus renounces all human greatness. He takes on the role of the servant, as in Isaiah 53, who gives himself 'for many'. And we take this for ourselves as we share in baptism and drink the cup of the Eucharist.

- *Pray to accept the humility of Christ into our own lives.*
- *Thank God for Jesus who stands for us with God and for God with us.*
- *Praise God for the gifts of baptism and Eucharist, joining us to himself.*

PROPER 25

(SUNDAY BETWEEN 23 AND 30 OCTOBER INCLUSIVE)

JOB 42.1–6, 10–17

In the old prose story of Job, within which the more sophisticated poem is enclosed, the conclusion is simple: to reinstate Job's wealth – on the grand scale. In the poem, Job accepts his place humbly before God's wonderful greatness (vv.1–6).

OR JEREMIAH 31.7–9
A promise of restoration for the exiled of Israel.

HEBREWS 7.23–28

The writer works out his image of Jesus as our 'high priest', shaped by the high priests of Israel. He has to use ingenuity, for the differences are as great as the parallels. Above all, Jesus is our mediator for always (as Psalm 110.4 foretold).

MARK 10.46B–52

The story of Bartimaeus is a beautiful picture of coming to faith – by need and by persistence; and the outcome is to follow Jesus with seeing eyes on his road to the Passion.

- *Pray to join the blind man in his cure and in his faith.*
- *How gladly we can praise the eternal stability of Jesus' work for our salvation.*
- *Pray for all whose 'blindness' before God is wilful and unnecessary.*

BIBLE SUNDAY

ISAIAH 55.1–11

The theme is the sheer generosity of God, like an abundant source of all provision for our lives. His goodness comes too in our inner lives, in forgiveness and in his utter faithfulness to us.

2 TIMOTHY 3.14—4.5

When this letter was written, perhaps 70 years after Jesus' lifetime, there was beginning to be a worry about believers straying from the received gospel message. Ever since, it has been a problem for Christian people, perhaps especially our leaders and teachers, needing sensitivity and care, lest faith should be bruised or stifled.

JOHN 5.36–47

Here, Jesus is put forward as the key to unlock the great meaning of scripture – the clue to what, taken as a whole, may seem unwieldy and obscure, as well as inspiring and feeding the soul. Without this key, we can easily go astray in our reading and pondering.

- *We give thanks for the gift of scripture and pray to read wisely and well.*

- *How can we read in the light of Christ?*

- *Pray for humility to receive from the Church just as we make our own contribution.*

DEDICATION FESTIVAL

(FIRST SUNDAY IN OCTOBER OR LAST SUNDAY AFTER TRINITY)

GENESIS 28.11–18

The story about Jacob at *bethel* ('house of God') serves as the early biblical prototype of places set apart for God – designated 'holy' and valued by believers.

OR REVELATION 21.9–14

It is not surprising that, in his poetic narrative of the place and time of ultimate perfection, the seer has in view a renewed holy city, marked with old signs of the presence of God.

1 PETER 2.1–10

This writer too draws on images relating to old Israel, with the stones of the holy city as the true people of God now known in Christ and his Church.

JOHN 10.22–29

Jesus is in the Temple in Jerusalem, where he stands as the unrecognized fulfilment of its role, above all as the true location of God among his own.

- *Grasp all signs and helpful symbols of the presence of God.*
- *Pray that holy places may retain their life-giving power.*
- *We praise God for 'temples' that have helped us in our Christian lives.*

ALL SAINTS' DAY (1 NOVEMBER)

See Year A, page 65.

ALL SAINTS' SUNDAY

See Year A, page 65.

FOURTH SUNDAY BEFORE ADVENT

DEUTERONOMY 6.1–9

This passage in the last book of the Law contains the central command to love God wholly, which (like others) Jesus highlighted.

HEBREWS 9.11–14

Taking elements of the old rules for sacrifices, the writer sees them as a picture of Jesus' self-giving and its effect for us.

MARK 12.28–34

Jesus takes up the two great commands – to love God and neighbour – and gives them unique force. Do they teach us all we need to know about duty?

- *Pray to grow in love for God.*
- *Praise God for our union with him through Christ.*
- *Does 'love' give us all the lead we need for the good life?*

THIRD SUNDAY BEFORE ADVENT

JONAH 3.1-5, 10

A story of God's ever-ready willingness to accept repentance.

HEBREWS 9.24-28

The writer takes the picture of the Jewish high priest's annual sacrifice for the sins of the people. It is taken up decisively and conclusively by Jesus, for us all.

MARK 1.14-20

The choice of followers and 'pupils' by Jesus sets the roots of the Church at the very start of his ministry. By many stumblings, they represent us all in accepting his call.

- *Pray to share the new disciples' readiness to abandon and to follow.*
- *We praise God for his open access to us, his people.*
- *We thank God for the gift and opportunity of his call to us.*

SECOND SUNDAY BEFORE ADVENT

DANIEL 12.1-3

The ancient Jews did not come to a clear belief in life after death until very late in the pre-Christian time. It may surprise us that its absence did not impair their trust in God. Here, from 167 BC, is one of the few witnesses to this belief. It came in terms of 'resurrection', renewed life as a pure gift from the hand of God.

HEBREWS 10.11-14 (15-18), 19-25

The picture is of the high priest in old Judaism entering the heart of the Temple, 'through the curtain', to offer the great sacrifice that would take away the people's sins. For the writer, it stands as a foreshadowing of Jesus, who also, we may say, 'went through' his own human life and death to the goal of heaven for us all.

MARK 13.1-8

Before his Passion, Jesus considers the Temple in Jerusalem and sees its transience. Its end will come and there will be much strife and confusion. Jews commonly saw such strife as the precursor to the coming of God's victory, and the contrast comes into Christian hopes – and fears.

- *Pray for a firmer hope in the great generosity of God.*
- *Give thanks for the binding gift of Jesus' self-offering.*
- *Can we accept the grief which often seems to be the essential gate to fulfilment?*

CHRIST THE KING

See Year A, page 69.

HARVEST FESTIVAL

See Year A, page 70.

FIRST SUNDAY OF ADVENT

JEREMIAH 33.14-16

The prophet, writing at a time of gloom and uncertainty, sees future joy in terms of a new king of the old house of David. In such a one lies hope of better things. Christians often came to make much of Jesus' having such an ancestry.

1 THESSALONIANS 3.9-13

This passage from the oldest of Paul's letters expresses movingly the apostle's affection and concern for his new gentile converts in Thessalonica in northern Greece. He has all the instincts of the true pastor, here on view from the very beginning of the Church's life.

LUKE 21.25-36

Each of the first three Gospels contains a vivid picture of the coming winding-up of the world with the return of Jesus in triumph and judgement. That early hope was not fulfilled, but the essential confidence in God which it expresses remains, even if we might put it less dramatically. But how do we feel it and know it?

- *Pray not to be so absorbed by the present that we cannot raise our eyes beyond.*

- *Thank God for the strength of Christian community which warms our hearts.*

- *Pray for the strengthening of confidence in God's future always open to us.*

SECOND SUNDAY OF ADVENT

BARUCH 5.1–9

In the spirit of the other later prophets, this passage speaks with joy and confidence of God's vindication of his people.

OR MALACHI 3.1–4

This late prophet of Israel looks forward to God's great day, with its dramatic force and frightening realism. No good underplaying the majesty of God's future in store for us. He is not to be trifled with and we must be watchful, always poised and alert before him.

PHILIPPIANS 1.3–11

Paul often began his letters with thanksgiving for the faith and love he saw in his converts. In this case, it is particularly heartfelt. He is in prison and Christians from Philippi have attended to his welfare. He is confident that their virtue will be rewarded.

LUKE 3.1–6

Luke the evangelist is a man with a feel for the world about him and he dates the start of Jesus' ministry carefully to AD 29 (as we call it, less cumbersomely than he had to do!). And that ministry begins with the ground-laying preaching of John the Baptist, full of promise for what is to come.

- *Vigilance before God is a quality we can easily forget.*
- *The warmth of Christian common life is to be cherished.*
- *Pray to sense the historical reality of Jesus' coming to his great work.*

THIRD SUNDAY OF ADVENT

ZEPHANIAH 3.14–20

The special strength of this passage from old Jewish prophecy lies in its stress of God being 'in your midst'. His presence is not just a hope for the future, but is recognized in the here and now. It is a confidence which early Christians were glad to share, with joy and excitement. So may we.

PHILIPPIANS 4.4–7

Familiar words, in liturgy and in musical settings. It is a passage of deep reassurance, coming remarkably from Paul in the midst of a time when he was in prison for his faith. His calm and confidence are worth dwelling upon.

LUKE 3.7–18

John does not simply baptize with a view to renewed service of God but also gives simple and direct moral instruction, appropriate to his audience. It is strictly practical, addressed to everyday temptations.

- *Pray to enter into a sense of God's real presence among us, not to be doubted.*
- *Pray for the ability to keep underlying serenity before God in the face of troubles.*
- *We hope not to neglect the simple duties that lie before us.*

FOURTH SUNDAY OF ADVENT

MICAH 5.2-5A

A passage seized upon in early Christianity in relation to Jesus' birth at Bethlehem, with its ancient associations with King David. It helped to kindle the hope of his saving role, if not political then certainly crucial in God's purposes, now seen afresh.

HEBREWS 10.5-10

A central theme of this writing is the way Jesus has superseded the crucial role in Judaism of the sacrifices in the Temple at Jerusalem, as ordered in the old Law of Moses. In his own very self, Jesus perfects all that they sought to do: the restoring of our relationship with God, spoiled by sin and the defects of our lives.

LUKE 1.39-45 (46-55)

The encounter between Mary and Elizabeth makes a familiar and beautiful scene, full of a sense of expectation of a wonderful future in store. Mary's song puts the hope into words. God seeks to transform human life at all levels and will achieve it by his generous gift.

- *Pray for the fulfilment of our dearest hopes in the life and meaning of Jesus.*
- *We trust that the offering of Jesus will stay in our hearts and minds.*
- *Trust that the encounter with Jesus may renew us at all levels of life with God.*

CHRISTMAS DAY AND EVENING OF CHRISTMAS EVE

See Year A, page 5.

FIRST SUNDAY OF CHRISTMAS

1 SAMUEL 2.18–20, 26

Samuel, dedicated from birth to the special service of God, makes a good
pattern for the child Jesus.

COLOSSIANS 3.12–17

Paul's teaching about the moral life is basic, plain – and joyful; not irksome,
harsh or burdensome.

LUKE 2.41–52

The boy Jesus devotes himself to the holy learning of his people – humbly and
devoutly.

- *Pray for the spirit of devout patience before God.*
- *Thank God for the daily joy of the service of God.*
- *Praise God for his loving guidance.*

SECOND SUNDAY OF CHRISTMAS

JEREMIAH 31.7-14

The prophet looks forward to the return from exile and humiliation of God's people. He gives a message of salvation and assurance which fills the hearers with gladness.

OR ECCLESIASTICUS 24.1-12

'Wisdom' was a symbol for God's loving purpose for his people: meaning that it was not frivolous or in the least irrational, but full of depth and sense.

EPHESIANS 1.3-14

Written in lofty and rather complex style, the passage outlines the process by which God promised and then brought about healing and redemption for his own through Christ.

JOHN 1.(1-9), 10-18

The second part of the prologue of the Gospel of John focuses on the reception of God's gift of himself in Jesus. He identified himself with us as an act of astonishing generosity – and blessed are those who receive and see.

- *Praise God for the assurance of his saving truth and the action to match it.*

- *We thank God for the whole saving drama enacted for us through Jesus.*

- *Pray that we may receive gladly the gift of God bestowed in Jesus.*

THE EPIPHANY

See Year A, page 8.

THE BAPTISM OF CHRIST

(FIRST SUNDAY OF EPIPHANY)

ISAIAH 43.1–7

God promises his loyalty to his people through all disasters, in particular captivity in distant parts.

ACTS 8.14–17

The conversion of Samaritans marks a first stage of the movement of the Church's mission beyond Jerusalem.

LUKE 3.15–17, 21–22

The baptism of Jesus is his commissioning for his unique role in the saving purpose of God.

- *Baptism is the sign of salvation, a foundation of hope.*
- *We praise God for the spread of the gospel from small beginnings.*
- *Thanks be to God for his faithfulness to his people.*

SECOND SUNDAY OF EPIPHANY

ISAIAH 62.1–5

We read of the joyful future promised to Israel, beloved by God, after the image of a marriage.

1 CORINTHIANS 12.1–11

There is to be nothing dull or monotonous about God's people: he inspires and provides a wide variety of gifts, united by the Spirit – and all vital, whether humdrum or spectacular.

JOHN 2.1–11

Jesus blesses the wedding with an abundance of good beyond all hope – it is a symbol of God's generosity to his people.

- *Pray for a sense of the vitality of the service of God.*
- *Thank God for the intimacy of love.*
- *Let us value all the gifts with which we may serve.*

THIRD SUNDAY OF EPIPHANY

NEHEMIAH 8.1–3, 8–10

When Jews returned from long and arduous captivity in Babylon in the sixth century before Christ, Ezra emerged as a leader, and presented them with God's book of the Law. It was their mark of identity – and was received with joy and gratitude.

1 CORINTHIANS 12.12–31A

Paul puts forward the vivid image of the Church as a body, all the parts co-operating and all equally essential to the life of the whole. So there is no room for friction and mutual disapproval or disagreement. They are all elements in a single community, all necessary, for the 'body' is that of Christ himself. He is their sole bond of unity.

LUKE 4.14–21

Luke gives us this passage at the start of Jesus' ministry in the world at large, and he begins in his own home town. The passage is then a kind of manifesto. Jesus stands for the care of the vulnerable and the giving of liberty. The message of Jesus is full of social and political implications – from the very start.

- *Pray to identify with those who seek liberty from captivity, whatever its kind.*

- *Thank God for the wide range of gifts available for the work of the gospel.*

- *How do we share in Jesus' ministry to the needy, the sick and those captive to whatever enslaving power?*

FOURTH SUNDAY OF EPIPHANY

EZEKIEL 43.27—44.4

Ezekiel is the prophet of a renewed Temple in Jerusalem, to be the sacrament of God's presence with his people. Christians today tend to be less wedded to the sheer mystique and holiness of their churches than in former times: the presence of God may be found in so many places, people and situations. But we can sense and value the great reverence which the passage evokes. It has its lessons for us to ponder.

1 CORINTHIANS 13.1–13

A passage that may be even over-familiar. In Paul's letter, it comes at a point where he is criticizing Christians who over-value their spiritual prowess, seeing themselves as above the ordinary ones who are less good at preaching or speaking with magical tongues. Paul says that the supreme gift is love; and he paints a picture of its character. It is wholly positive and geared towards the good of all.

LUKE 2.22–40

Observing a rite prescribed in the Jewish law, Jesus' parents take him to the Temple in Jerusalem. It turns out to be an event where his whole mission is foreseen and he is dedicated for its fulfilment. He will bring the light of God to all peoples.

- *Pray to recognize and value the presence of God wherever it may come to us.*
- *Praise God for the gift of love and constantly reflect on its character and demands.*
- *May we reflect upon the scene that sets out the mission lying ahead of Jesus.*

THE PRESENTATION OF CHRIST

(2 FEBRUARY)

See Year A, page 13.

FIFTH SUNDAY OF EPIPHANY

ISAIAH 6.1–8 (9–13)

The angel's words experienced by the prophet in the Temple at Jerusalem have become some of the most solemn in Christian worship. After all, we long to be united with the worship of heaven and to give ourselves in love to God. It is a picture above all of holiness, the sense of God's 'otherness', that puts us in our little place and reduces us to silence before him.

1 CORINTHIANS 15.1–11

Here Paul gives us the earliest statement of the content of Christian belief – and he himself had received it from those who were believers before him. It is as elementary as we could wish: that Christ died 'for our sins', giving himself to God for us; that he was buried; and that he was raised to new life, vindicated by God. And Paul is among God's apostles or agents – for our ultimate good. He felt he was lucky to have scraped in!

LUKE 5.1–11

Mysteriously, Jesus calls whom he will and does it so wonderfully as to convey his unique role. Peter is humbled and responds in penitence. It is a picture of how coming to faith might be, in its essence, for any of us.

- *Pray to grow in the experience of God's sheer holiness, utterly other than ourselves.*
- *Thank God for the simplicity at the heart of faith.*
- *The 'call' of God is always mysterious, for each of us. Pray to welcome it.*

SIXTH SUNDAY OF EPIPHANY

JEREMIAH 17.5-10

Our tendency may be to revere God our Creator and to see him in the setting of 'everything that exists'. But the other side of faith in God is to see his 'otherness'. He is wholly beyond and unlike everything else. To trust in him is to know that which is quite different, quite beyond our ordinary ways of thinking and knowing. Only so can we cease to be 'devious'.

1 CORINTHIANS 15.12-20

The Christians of Corinth were worried that some among them were dying before Christ's expected return. Do not worry, says Paul; to be 'in Christ' is to be wholly secure. And we who are his shall be 'like him'; and we are safe in God's life-giving love for all his people.

LUKE 6.17-26

Here is Luke's version of the more familiar 'Sermon on the Mount' as found in Matthew. In some ways it is simpler and more down to earth. God's blessing is for the poor, the hungry and the sad, in the ordinary senses of the words. And there is 'woe' on those who enjoy life's good things (as we so oddly name them). Is it necessary to know deprivation in some way truly to be ready to love God?

- *Pray for simplicity in our sense of God.*
- *Can we learn to trust God, for life and for death, in all simplicity?*
- *Pray to be ready to go against natural instincts for the sake of grasping the message of Jesus.*

SEVENTH SUNDAY OF EPIPHANY

GENESIS 45.3–11, 15

Joseph, having become great in Egypt, is reconciled to his brothers who had sold him into slavery. The whole saga has misery and redemption as its running theme.

1 CORINTHIANS 15.35–38, 42–50

Paul seeks to explain the nature of the 'bodies' which will be ours at resurrection day. It is a theory not without difficulties, but Paul assures his Christians of God's true future for his own.

LUKE 6.27–38

Jesus teaches the most lavish and carefree generosity. We are to be open-hearted beyond all normal reason.

- *How generous are we ready to be?*
- *Pray to trust God through all ills, even death.*
- *Thank God for the gift of reconciliation.*

SECOND SUNDAY BEFORE LENT

GENESIS 2.4B–9, 15–25

This passage should be read as a more story-like account of creation than the more formal one in Genesis 1. It is a vivid picture of the paradise we are meant for: humans are at its centre.

REVELATION 4

We are given an extravagant and astonishing picture of the worship of heaven. And the writer, poet and seer, is admitted to witness it. The ingredients of the picture come from the Jewish tradition for thinking of the wonder of God. Our proper response is to enter into the picture with humble amazement.

LUKE 8.22–25

Jesus is Master not only of human life, with its sicknesses and weaknesses, both physical and moral, but also of nature itself. In this story we see him acting as Adam did in Eden, in charge of the world in its threatening disorder. And the proper human response is trust at the deepest level.

- *May the love of God move us to worship that truly captures us.*
- *Pray to grow in trust of God, whatever comes our way.*
- *Can we recapture the wonder of God's creative gift?*

SUNDAY NEXT BEFORE LENT

EXODUS 34.29–35

The veil that covered Moses' face on coming away from God's presence has been a source of great fascination to artists and poets down the centuries. Perhaps it was to shield ordinary mortals from the direct impact of God's glory transmitted via Moses. We can see that point, whatever we think of the story itself. We are as nothing before God's reality.

2 CORINTHIANS 3.12—4.2

Paul had his own sense of the story in Exodus 34. The veil was to prevent our seeing how Moses' face lost its shining quality as he was longer away from God's direct presence. That decline and loss was itself a symbol of the temporary quality of the whole of the 'old covenant' – which Moses stood for. In contrast, the light of Christ grows stronger than ever, and it shines upon and through us who belong to him.

LUKE 9.28B–36 (37–43)

The story of the Transfiguration of Jesus in the presence of his leading disciples strikes some as strange, others as wonderful in its mystery and splendour. It may be seen as a foreshadowing of the resurrection, already in the course of Jesus' life. It is a glimpse of his true character and destiny even when he is living life among us.

- *How can we grow in our sense of God being quite 'other' than anything we can conceive?*
- *Yet we give thanks that in Christ we are enabled to 'draw near' to him.*
- *Pray to see God's glorious reality even in the midst of the humdrum.*

ASH WEDNESDAY

JOEL 2.1–2, 12–17

The prophet calls on God's people to observe the holy time with all solemnity. It binds all together in the strict, heartfelt service of God.

OR ISAIAH 58.1–12
God speaks via the prophet in exasperation at superficial religion. True service of God lies not in ritual acts but in care for the needy, bringing joy for all.

2 CORINTHIANS 5.20B—6.10

Paul sets out his credentials as Christ's ambassador. They lie in the trials he has endured – leading to all the many blessings of the gospel of Christ.

MATTHEW 6.1–6, 16–21

Religious observance can be done for absurd reasons, even to win the approval of other people. Purity of motive is required – for the love of God.

OR JOHN 8.1–11
We are not to sin – but equally, we must not be censorious, in effect putting ourselves on a pedestal of virtue. How wickedly foolish!

- *Pray for purity in our love of God.*

- *The gift of Lent is to deepen our true service.*

- *Thank God for the chance to grow in love.*

FIRST SUNDAY OF LENT

DEUTERONOMY 26.1–11

We hear a passage in which Israel is recalled to the fundamentals of the nation's creed: the act of rescue from slavery in Egypt which we call the Exodus. The joy to which it led ('a land flowing with milk and honey') reminds us of the basic gifts we have received through Christ, the awareness of our being received anew by God.

ROMANS 10.8B–13

One of the early Christians' great convictions (perhaps Paul above all) was the universal scope of their message. It was for everybody, regardless of race or nation. Also it was an accessible message, the simple offer of love from God, seeking response.

LUKE 4.1–13

Lent began the time of preparation of candidates for their baptism at Easter, but it soon came to be seen as foreshadowed in Jesus' time of testing in the wilderness before embarking on his ministry. It has long been for Christians an annual time of penitence, their own 'testing', with fasting strongly to the fore. In the face of his testing, Jesus emerges unscathed. May we do the same!

- *Pray never to lose sight of the fundamentals of faith and relationship with God.*

- *Thank God for the universal character of the Christian message.*

- *May we keep our sense of 'testing' before God and so of growth towards him.*

SECOND SUNDAY OF LENT

GENESIS 15.1–12, 17–18

The story of Abraham, founding father of Israel, is one of salvation by the skin of the teeth. At every point it hangs by a thread – and the generous fidelity of God wins through despite everything. Christians soon saw this story as pointing to God's act in Jesus. There too God's universal purpose of good was channelled through this fragile channel, so easily ruined.

PHILIPPIANS 3.17—4.1

Paul is a strong pastor of his people, leading from the front. And his eyes are on 'heaven', the place or sphere where Christians truly belong and where they see their destiny – as distinct from Rome or any other earthly place of loyalty.

LUKE 13.31–35

The place of Jerusalem in early Christian feeling and loyalty was one of great pain and difficulty. It remained a place of 'belonging'; yet it was where Jesus had been executed, at the hands of those who ruled it. The double feeling has remained in Christian consciousness to this day.

- *Pray not to presume upon God's goodness but to wonder always at his love for us.*

- *Pray to see our goal, already assured, in God himself.*

- *Thank God for holy places, but see them all as pointing beyond themselves.*

THIRD SUNDAY OF LENT

ISAIAH 55.1–9

The prophet issues a call to follow the real and not the sham – and to follow without delay, for there is urgency where our relations with God are concerned. God is beyond our imagining, and we must not take him for granted.

1 CORINTHIANS 10.1–13

Paul seeks shadowy parallels to Christian Baptism and Eucharist in episodes in the story of Israel's wanderings in the wilderness on the way from Egypt to the land of promise. The message is one of warning: do not presume on God's goodness, but be ready and armed to survive any testing that may come one's way.

LUKE 13.1–9

Jesus gives a stern warning of the need for repentance. It is not popular and perhaps we should say it is not quite moral for exhortation to be backed up by threats. But there is something to be said for letting realism have its head, lest we fall into complacency.

- *Pray never to take God for granted, but to stay open to his call.*
- *Pray to be armed against the threats of wrong thinking and doing, for the sake of God's love.*
- *Pray to be armed against all dangers of complacency.*

FOURTH SUNDAY OF LENT

JOSHUA 5.9–12

You might read this little episode as a kind of picture of the small-scale festivity of 'Refreshment Sunday' in the middle of Lent.

2 CORINTHIANS 5.16–21

Christ brings not just new thoughts about God and ourselves, not just a new depth of relationship with God, but, says Paul, a whole new start – new creation.

LUKE 15.1–3, 11B–32

The Story of the Prodigal Son, as we name it, would be more fairly called the Story of the Loving Father, for he, in his God-like role, is the one who wins our devotion.

- *We do not have to qualify to receive God's love.*
- *Praise God for the new world we experience in Christ.*
- *God's generosity to us is without limit and without conditions.*

MOTHERING SUNDAY

See Year A, page 24.

FIFTH SUNDAY OF LENT

(PASSIONTIDE BEGINS)

ISAIAH 43.16–21

The prophet recalls the great foundation story of Israel, the liberation from slavery in Egypt and the crossing of the Red Sea. But then, surprisingly, he puts that behind him and looks forward to a greater future when God will bring all things to a wonderful perfection, beyond imagining.

PHILIPPIANS 3.4B–14

Paul really takes off in this passage. He asserts his proud credentials as a Jew, including his membership of the strict guild of the Pharisees. Then the contrast. All this he had gladly renounced for the sake of Christ, whose people he had despised and persecuted. It was a revolution. He had come to see his right relationship with God as wholly dependent on his commitment to Christ. That was itself pure gift from God.

JOHN 12.1–8

All the Gospels, except that of Luke, have the story of a woman anointing Jesus at the opening of the narrative of the Passion. They differ in detail, but all emphasize – and applaud – the extravagance of her action and so of her devotion. It is a shock to those of puritanical instincts, and not very Lenten. But at the start of Passiontide, it warns us against negative approaches to Jesus' death and takes us into the fervent love for God which that death is to stir in us. To absorb its deep generosity is worth everything we can offer.

- *Dare to aim high in loyalty to God.*
- *Be ready to expect new depths and heights in your relationship with God: 'new thoughts of God, new hopes of heaven'.*
- *God is always a step ahead of what we have so far known of him. How can we follow?*

PALM SUNDAY

(LITURGY OF THE PASSION)

ISAIAH 50.4–9A

This passage is about an anonymous victim of persecution who does not waver in his trust in God. From early times, Christians have seen in it a foreshadowing of Jesus' suffering. Notice the power of the victim's non-resistance – both towards the tormentors and towards the persecution itself. He can even see his suffering as a gift from God, the route to great good. So it is with Jesus.

PHILIPPIANS 2.5–11

This passage is thought to be an early Christian hymn. Paul puts it into his letter as a summary of the faith, in effect an early creed. Perhaps we should think of all creeds as 'hymns' – not sort-of-legal statements but poetic acts of praise to God. The hymn tells of the extreme humility of Christ's act in putting aside his heavenly status and in accepting human life at its most degraded. His triumphant reward is the source of our own confidence in God.

LUKE 22.14—23.56 OR LUKE 23.1–49

Luke depicts Christ's final hours as a kind of sermon to move our hearts and nourish our characters. In his extremity, he shows three exemplary qualities. First, he asks for the forgiveness of those who put him to death. Second, from the cross itself he makes his last convert, the penitent thief. Third, he dies with assured surrender of himself to God, as son to father. And, rightly, the crowds of bystanders are moved.

- *Good comes out of evil, especially when we accept its onslaught.*
- *It is in venturing all, that we have the chance of the greater gain to our inner selves.*
- *We may do most good in bad times by steadfastly holding to the course of generosity.*

MAUNDY THURSDAY

See Year A, page 27.

GOOD FRIDAY

See Year A, page 28.

EASTER DAY

ISAIAH 65.17–25

In a lovely, poetic passage, the prophet tells of his vision of a new world, where all will be at peace and we shall live in contentment – paradise indeed.

1 CORINTHIANS 15.19–26

Paul's converts have what to us may seem an unlikely distortion of faith. They think of themselves as already, in their inner selves, 'risen' completely to new life – no longer part of ordinary human society. No, says Paul, there is always a greater future ahead of us, however wonderful what is already ours. And on that future we must keep our eyes. Here, he tells how he thinks it will work out for the world; but God's ultimate triumph is the key point for faith. In the meantime, we are 'on the way', serving God in the here and now.

OR ACTS 10.34–43

Peter gives a summary of the story of the salvation brought by Jesus, but the crucial point here is the universal scope of that work; it is for gentiles as well as for Jews. A major step in the Church's life and the spread of the good news.

JOHN 20.1–18

Two stories of Easter Day, telling first of the abandoned tomb and then of Jesus' meeting with Mary Magdalene. A new world is born and the old is put behind. And love and recognition are the marks of the new.

OR LUKE 24.1–12

All the Gospels have a version of this story of Easter morning, where women are the first witnesses of the deserted tomb. In our day, people seem often to be greatly attached to the graves and corpses and body-parts of their loved ones. So it is good to remember that, with and like our Lord, we are bigger and more important than that earthly level of things. What matters is the God-given greatness of what we are for and what we add up to.

- *Pray for boldness to stretch up to God's purpose for you. No virtue in false humility.*

- *Pray to recognize the greater future that always lies ahead for each of us.*

- *Amazement is a great quality to cultivate in our relationship with God.*

SECOND SUNDAY OF EASTER

EXODUS 14.10-31; 15.20-21

The Israelites try to flee their Egyptian captors. All is in the balance: will they get away or not? With God's help, success is assured.

OR ACTS 5.27-32

Like the other speeches in Acts, by apostles and others, this one is a brief summary of the Christian message. What was new – and offensive – about the new faith was its centring on Jesus. His life, his shameful death and amazing resurrection represented a new direction in God's gift of himself to his people. And novelty is rarely the route to popularity.

REVELATION 1.4-8

The author of the Book of Revelation opens with letters to seven Christian congregations in towns in Asia Minor (modern Turkey), for whom he writes his book. It echoes words about Israel in Exodus 19 ('he made us a kingdom of priests') and speaks of their marvellous new status – now close to God and his chosen ones, because of Jesus' victory.

JOHN 20.19-31

Some Christians identify easily with Thomas' hesitations, others are inclined to regret them. But there is room, it seems, for both kinds of response. And John offers his Gospel with the single aim of bringing us, by whatever means, to 'life in his name'.

- *At its heart, is Christian faith a matter of simple allegiance or something more complicated?*

- *We believe without having 'seen'. Can we rejoice in that?*

- *The demands of faith are sometimes grievous. Are we ready for them?*

THIRD SUNDAY OF EASTER

ZEPHANIAH 3.14-20

The prophet foresees, exuberantly, a time of fulfilment when all shall be well.

OR ACTS 9.1-6 (7-20)

We read the story of Paul's conversion from being a persecutor of Jesus' followers to becoming not just a simple Christian but the one who opened the Church up freely to non-Jews. It was the first key turning-point in the history of the Church – and we still live in the light of it.

REVELATION 5.11-14

The vision of John makes one thing abundantly clear: the priority of worship in the scheme of things. It is the offering due from all creation to God and to Christ, crucified and now vindicated.

JOHN 21.1-19

This is a story about recognition. We know the Lord in the sharing of the gift of his ever-nourishing bread. And then a story about the work from him that follows. Recognition leads to service and even to death.

- *Past turning-points are gifts of God that make all the difference.*

- *Worship is the basis on which all Christian 'following' rests.*

- *Pray for readiness to recognize the call of God, and then to respond.*

FOURTH SUNDAY OF EASTER

GENESIS 7.1–5, 11–18; 8.6–18; 9.8–13

The story of the Flood and Noah's safe passage can stand as a symbol of salvation against the odds.

OR ACTS 9.36–43

Peter performs a miracle that reminds us of the acts of Jesus. The writer of Acts wants us to see that, unique as Jesus was, his followers do not live simply on memories of a great time past, but as servants of the living God and the present Lord.

REVELATION 7.9–17

As always, John's vision of heaven is one of worship. Here, the worshippers centre on those who have suffered martyrdom for their faith in Christ. Such suffering is the keenest test of the reality of commitment. Since that early time, martyrs have always had a place of special honour among Christian people, as the sharpest reminders of the total difference that faith must make.

JOHN 10.22–30

There comes a point when no more can be done to bring about faith – in ourselves or in others. We 'see' or we fail to see. But to have come to faith is the key to the fullness of our relationship with God, and colours everything about us at all levels.

- *The Church lives now as the people of God in the present time, not in a mist of nostalgia.*

- *Suffering of one kind or another has always been the hallmark of faith.*

- *Pray to know the stability of our life in Christ – and yet be ever on the move.*

FIFTH SUNDAY OF EASTER

ACTS 11.1–18

From time to time the Church faces a major decision, as recently over women's ordination. The earliest such issue was on the question whether, if you were a gentile, to be a Christian entailed first becoming a Jew – in broader terms, what it means to say that the Christian gospel *fulfils* Judaism. Does it mean *supersede* or *build upon*? If it had not been settled in a liberal way, life might still be very different for us all.

OR BARUCH 3.9–15, 32–36; 4.1–4
The prophet paints a familiar picture: of Israel's duty to obey God's will and follow his teaching.

OR GENESIS 22.1–18
The dramatic and terrifying story of the near death of Isaac by God's command. Abraham is steadfast in faith and the boy is spared. Christians have seen it as a sort of sign of the giving of Jesus: see Romans 8.32.

REVELATION 21.1–6

Revelation draws towards its close with a wonderful vision of how everything must surely end up: in beautiful perfection, with heaven and earth renewed, all that is negative banished and all things summed up in the love of God. Nothing less can satisfy.

JOHN 13.31–35

Love, in the Gospel of John, is the cement that binds together the Christian community. In this Gospel as a whole we have no other command of Jesus. It is as if we are being told: love one another truly, and you will judge aright on other moral issues. We are put on trust, and it is a risky business!

- *For the Church to do the right things, is it enough to stick to the past?*

- *To do right now, we should have a vision for the future.*

- *Pray to love so purely that good judgement will follow.*

SIXTH SUNDAY OF EASTER

ACTS 16.9-15

This passage tells of a momentous development in the spread of Christianity. For the first time Paul moves to what was already called Europe. He comes to Philippi, in northern Greece, and in the rest of the chapter we can read of the imprisonment he suffers – and of the conversion of the jailer, followed by his baptism, along with his family. It is the first instance we have for the baptism of small children: a big landmark in our history.

OR EZEKIEL 37.1-14
The famous image of the dry bones that came together and live is well known as a parable for the revitalizing power of the Christian gospel.

REVELATION 21.10, 22—22.5

This beautiful vision of the new world that embodies God's perfection uses poetic themes familiar from the Old Testament. Jerusalem the holy city of God, the centre of God's world; the tree of life in Eden; God seen as wonderful and glorious light. The old images grow and are transformed in the Christian poet's pen.

JOHN 14.23-29

Jesus promises the Spirit as the continuer of his own presence: in other words, God's saving work will not slacken.

OR JOHN 5.1-9
This is one of the few stories in the Gospel of John that remind us of the other Gospels, with their many tales of Jesus' healings of the sick. Archaeology has discovered the site that is here described.

- *Thanks for our Christian past is surely a good thought and prayer to nourish.*
- *So too, by contrast, is a lively hope for the future perfection that God wills.*
- *Jesus the healer is a signal and guarantee of that hope.*

ASCENSION DAY

See Year A, page 35.

SEVENTH SUNDAY OF EASTER

(SUNDAY AFTER ASCENSION DAY)

ACTS 16.16–34

This striking story contains the earliest reference to children being baptized. It happens to the jailer at Philippi 'and his entire family'. In each of the amazing stories in Acts, we meet the breaking of some patch of new ground in the Christian mission. So the message began its extraordinary spread, first across the Mediterranean world: here to Greece (indeed, to Europe for the first time).

OR EZEKIEL 36.24–28
The theme is restoration and homecoming, one that recurs in the Old Testament. Here, it centres on the Land of Israel – a foretaste of heaven.

REVELATION 22.12–14, 16–17, 20–21

The final passage of Revelation is ecstatic in its use of the strong image of Jesus and his people as bridegroom and bride, united by love and longing and by the desire for fulfilment of every hope.

JOHN 17.20–26

This chapter of the Gospel of John is a prayer of Jesus to God, whereby his followers are united with God through him. It expresses the intensity of the relationship that he establishes in the union of a single love.

- *The taking root of the Christian faith is liable to be in unforeseen ways.*
- *We long for the consummation of the relationship with God which Jesus gives to us.*
- *Pray for readiness to receive the love of God in all its depth.*

DAY OF PENTECOST

ACTS 2.1–21

The Holy Spirit means God as powerfully involved among us – and the story gives a striking example of such power that has made its mark on the Christian imagination, especially in its promise of universality.

OR GENESIS 11.1–9
The story gave an explanation for the rich variety of human language – impeding mutual understanding. Pentecost is depicted as a miraculous reversal of Babel's confusion. Under God, we can find unity.

ROMANS 8.14–17

For Paul, 'the Spirit' signifies God at work now, in the present, in the lives of those who love and serve him. It is the sign and the spur for our union with God.

JOHN 14.8–17 (25–27)

For John's Gospel, the Spirit is a way of assuring us that the time of Jesus was not an all-time 'high' the like of which we can never see again. On the contrary, 'the Spirit' means that what Jesus was and did then is still true and available for his own.

- *The Christian message soon broke free of its original bounds. It is universal in its scope.*
- *The Spirit is the gift of God's presence and the sign of our hope.*
- *Pray to live in the present as the gift of our loving and powerful God.*

TRINITY SUNDAY

PROVERBS 8.1–4, 22–31

Old Jewish poetry used the image of God's 'wisdom', seen as his beloved companion and agent in the creation of everything. It was a way of expressing the belief that the world was at root an intelligible and orderly design of God – not a chaotic or random place, where things can go anyhow. Experience might point us either way, and Proverbs reassures us.

ROMANS 5.1–5

This passage is at the heart of Paul's vision of Christian faith. Christ's coming means that we are freely and with bountiful grace accepted and empowered by God – not because we deserve it but because he loves us.

JOHN 16.12–15

We sometimes speak as if there were on the one hand Jesus, with his message and his example, and then, on the other hand, the Holy Spirit, less defined in our minds but certainly different. Not so. The Spirit is simply a way of speaking of the permanent and ever-fresh legacy of Christ among us. God is not divided, but is ever new in his coming to us.

- *The creation is made by God's wisdom. It is a thought that is both the deepest root of modern science and also of our struggle to make sense of the world around us. We do not live in a haphazard chaos.*

- *Is it not our greatest reassurance to know that God accepts and restores us because he loves us, not because of our fitful efforts?*

- *Jesus is the true picture of God in human terms once and, with endless variation, for ever.*

CORPUS CHRISTI/THANKSGIVING FOR HOLY COMMUNION

See Year A, page 39.

PROPER 3

ECCLESIASTICUS 27.4–7

A gloomy, even bilious (also snobby!) recipe for human judging of one's fellows. Why is it set?

OR ISAIAH 55.10–13
A confident statement of the power of God's 'word'; that is, his disposing of the world's affairs.

1 CORINTHIANS 15.51–58

Paul ends his long discussion of 'resurrection' in response to problems among some Christians in Corinth. He gives a ringing statement of his faith in God's future for his people.

LUKE 6.39–49

Jesus enjoins humility and awareness of one's own faults. But the need for integrity of soul and conduct is in the forefront.

- *Pray for faith in the new life that God offers to us in Christ.*
- *We need candour about ourselves if we are to grow in virtue.*
- *Do we believe in God who can make all things new?*

PROPER 4

1 KINGS 18.20–21 (22–29), 30–39

Elijah shows himself a doughty fighter for the cause of Israel's Yahweh, against the other deities favoured by the authorities of the time. As usual Yahweh, via Elijah, wins.

OR 1 KINGS 8.22–30, 41–43
Solomon, the great King of Israel, who had built the Temple in Jerusalem, solemnly celebrates Israel's arrival as a great power in the region.

GALATIANS 1.1–12

Paul is appalled by the fact that his gentile converts are being subverted by law-observing Jewish Christians from the pure and free gospel he had taught them. What can they possibly hope to gain?

LUKE 7.1B–10

In the ancient world, numerous non-Jews felt attracted to Judaism – by its monotheism and its strong morality. Acts shows such people being among the early converts to Christianity, and here Jesus and the centurion foreshadow that development.

- *How important is it to stick to true religion?*
- *We thank God for the gospel that we have received.*
- *Pray to join breadth of mind and heart with devotion to the quest for God's truth.*

⋅PROPER 5

1 KINGS 17.8–16 (17–24)

Elijah the prophet gives miraculous succour to a vulnerable woman and her son.

GALATIANS 1.11–24

Paul's own account of his conversion: he describes it as an inner revelation of Christ, and it was also his call to the role of 'apostle' or emissary of Christ to non-Jews. But in due course he did make contact with the Church's existing leaders, Peter and James.

LUKE 7.11–17

For a widow to lose her son was a tragedy indeed in the world of the time – not just emotional disaster but economic ruin. Jesus rescues them from the depths, like Elijah of old.

- *Pray for those who endure tragedy.*
- *Praise God for the work of Paul the apostle.*
- *Pray for all who undertake apostolic work.*

PROPER 6

(SUNDAY BETWEEN 12 AND 18 JUNE INCLUSIVE, IF AFTER TRINITY SUNDAY)

1 KINGS 21.1B–10 (11–14), 15–21A

The story of Naboth's vineyard resonates in every society at every time. Once, such exploitation of the weaker by the stronger could (if you were very bold) be seen as an offence against God's righteousness. Now, we deal with it as an affront to human rights and go to the courts. Progress?

OR 2 SAMUEL 11.26—12.10, 13–15
It is a story of gross sin and abuse of power by David – and the prophet wins his confession.

GALATIANS 2.15–21

Paul deals with the grave issue facing Christians of his time and his circle. Must a Christian be a Jew as the basis of his or her identity? No, thunders Paul, cutting through any such ideas. Christ is all-embracing and all-sufficient as our route to God. Anything further merely blurs the truth.

LUKE 7.36—8.3

Jesus proclaims the need for only penitence and loving devotion if we are to come to God. Mere correctness, especially if grudgingly offered, gets us nowhere, however respectable it is thought to be.

- *Social justice is inside, not outside, the concerns of God.*
- *We should keep hold of the simple essentials of Christian allegiance.*
- *Pray never to lose the sense of directness in our relationship with God.*

PROPER 7

1 KINGS 19.1–4 (5–7), 8–15A

This is one of the great stories about Elijah, the out-of-line prophet who stuck to his guns at great cost to his comfort. He was no friend to the authorities, but his assurance came from God, made known not in great and noisy signs but in the 'sound of sheer silence'.

OR ISAIAH 65.1–9
The prophet wears the mantle of God, whose servant he is, and expresses anguish at the neglect of God and the sheer treachery that he sees in Israel.

GALATIANS 3.23–29

This passage gives us one of Paul's more positive thoughts about God's gift of the Jewish Law through Moses long ago. It was a kind of stern childminder in the time of our immaturity. Nevertheless, says Paul, its day is now over. Taken over 'into Christ', we are mature – and more, our background is irrelevant. Race, gender and class no longer divide us; for Christ unites us all, whoever we are.

LUKE 8.26–39

To most modern people, this is not one of the most congenial Gospel stories. We have to realize that, in the first century, people saw what we call serious mental illness as the result of possession by evil spirits, agents of Satan; and they were not strong on animal rights. To such conditions, as to other ills, Jesus brings healing and new order, but at a disturbing cost.

- *Does it ring bells to experience God as 'the sound of sheer silence'?*
- *How much is the cause of sheer righteousness worth to us?*
- *Does the Church (do we) succeed in believing that we are 'all one in Christ Jesus'?*

PROPER 8

2 KINGS 2.1–2, 6–14

The mantle of 'prophet of Israel' is handed over as Elijah is taken up to heaven. (And the English language acquired a metaphor, to use in less dramatic circumstances.)

OR 1 KINGS 19.15–16, 19–21

As in many societies, so in ancient Israel, the 'holy man' was an ambiguous figure, mysteriously attractive because he had the gift of speaking truth and doing right without fudging; but also forbidding and frightening because he told you what you would prefer not to hear and to do what you would rather leave undone. No wonder Elisha hesitated. See the Gospel below for the same principle still at work.

GALATIANS 5.1, 13–25

Paul was a great advocate of freedom, but he did not mean liberty to do as all our impulses tell us. The pressure of God leads us to find our freedom in all kinds of splendid single-minded virtue, united in our purpose on behalf of God.

LUKE 9.51–62

Echoing the story of Elijah's summons to Elisha, Luke tells how Jesus' call gave no room for hesitation. And it was a call not to ease but to strenuous 'following', even to death; and certainly it flew in the face of ordinary customs and expectations of humdrum duty. So it was and so it may still be.

- *First we admire Elijah and his like, then we wonder how far we can travel along their road.*

- *Pray for the gift of single-mindedness at the heart of life.*

- *The search for our true liberty is constant; we can do worse things with our time than concentrate on its demands.*

PROPER 9

(SUNDAY BETWEEN 3 AND 9 JULY INCLUSIVE)

2 KINGS 5.1–14

The VIP of a neighbouring kingdom has the pride of nation and of class. But humility won the day – and Naaman became devoted to Yahweh.

OR ISAIAH 66.10–14
The last 11 chapters of the Book of Isaiah have a character of their own. They are full of visionary hope and of trust that God will bring delight and prosperity to his people. So the swing between a sense of God's righteous judgement and his love for his own comes to rest on the side of acceptance and welcome.

GALATIANS 6.(1–6), 7–16

Paul wrote Galatians in a state of great upset that his mission to gentiles, based on single-minded devotion to Christ and reliance on him as God's all-sufficient gift to us, was being blurred by Jewish Christians who wanted to impose obedience to the Jewish law. Paul will have none of it and sees it as a matter of the deepest principle. Having dictated most of the letter to a secretary, he takes up a furious pen himself for the final lines.

LUKE 10.1–11, 16–20

Luke tells of missions in Galilee and neighbouring, less purely Jewish territory, during Jesus' ministry, and he conveys an atmosphere of great freshness and hope. We can argue how appropriate nowadays is the attitude of 'take it or leave it' – which has its modern imitators of course. Others prefer to discuss and ponder. Is that letting the side down?

- *A vision of how good everything could be is perhaps a spur to collaborating with God's cause.*

- *Is Paul's single-mindedness always better than compromise? Or does it depend on the case?*

- *Christian mission looks different in a multicultural society. What might that do to us? And where does godly wisdom lie?*

PROPER 10

(SUNDAY BETWEEN 10 AND 16 JULY INCLUSIVE)

AMOS 7.7-17

The prophet's message is found intolerable by its hearers: he is too candid, too threatening to authorities. And Amos is dismissed by the powers that be.

OR DEUTERONOMY 30.9-14

The Book of Deuteronomy presupposes a rural society, and the atmosphere of a harvest festival is never far away. But in this passage the stress falls on the closeness of God, especially in the precious gift of the pattern of life that he lays down.

COLOSSIANS 1.1-14

The opening of this letter is full of thankfulness for the gifts of God that flow from Christ and are now available to those who will receive them. The essence is a new relationship of peace and hope, in a new context altogether – 'the kingdom of his dear Son'.

LUKE 10.25-37

The point of the story is not quite as obvious as it seems. The priest and Levite were correct – according to their lights; for the Law forbade pollution by attending to a possible corpse. The Samaritan's triumph is in going beyond any demand that his society could make of him – where loving your neighbour meant caring for those of your own community, and why should a heretical and rejected Samaritan (as seen in orthodox Jewish eyes) care for those not of his own kind? In fact he leaps over the boundary – and finds heroic truth and goodness.

- *How ready is our generosity to go beyond easy or conventional bounds (the goodness of the flag-day contribution)?*

- *Can we recapture the greatness of what God has done to reconstruct our whole standing in life?*

- *How should we be looking at life if God had not touched us for good?*

PROPER 11

(SUNDAY BETWEEN 17 AND 23 JULY INCLUSIVE)

AMOS 8.1–12

Amos was what we would call a social reformer, to the point of being a fire-brand and a nuisance, exposing injustice – and striking a new note for our sense of God's will.

OR GENESIS 18.1–10A

The passage is familiar as depicted in the Russian icons which see the three heavenly visitors as a foreshadowing of the Trinity, as in later Christian belief. It is God himself who brings to Abraham a promise of a son (Isaac), so guaranteeing at last his being the father and source of God's people.

COLOSSIANS 1.15–28

The first six verses of the passage may well be an early Christian hymn, expressing belief about Christ in high poetic language. He is nothing less than the comprehensive expression of God to us humans, in every way and from every point of view. So how marvellous to have received this divine mystery ('secret'), now at last revealed.

LUKE 10.38–42

This lovely little story has often seized the Christian imagination. It is seen as setting side by side practical service and life dedicated to prayer. There is little doubt where Jesus places the weight.

- *The story of Isaac's birth reminds us how much may hang by a single thread. So it was with the self-offering of Jesus, and so it may be in our own lives.*

- *Christ meets us in all dimensions and sides of our existence – and once it is given, there is no limit to his generosity.*

- *A good question: how to balance (is that the right word?) the demands of service to others and love for God? Is it a live choice – if faith is true? Or can the two coincide?*

PROPER 12

(SUNDAY BETWEEN 24 AND 30 JULY INCLUSIVE)

HOSEA 1.2–10

The prophet vividly expresses his teaching in the make-up of his family. His message combines severe criticism with words of hope.

OR GENESIS 18.20–32

The story is irresistible for its quality of suspense. But it presents God in a light that may now seem primitive or unworthy. Abraham is bargaining with God and presenting what we may see as a more moral stance than God himself. But we may reflect that his ways are not always necessarily the same as ours would be or ought to be. Wisdom can be many-layered.

COLOSSIANS 2.6–15 (16–19)

Paul is glad that the old Jewish criteria for membership of God's people have gone. In the new situation, there can be no compromise with God's fresh provision. Christ suffices and he stands alone as far as Christians are concerned in their relating to God.

LUKE 11.1–13

God is generous – totally so. But we have no business to take him for granted and we must stick to him like leeches. He is no milch-cow, no 'soft touch'.

- *Can we manage to believe that Christ is all and needs no support, no other force?*

- *Are there deeper ways of thinking of prayer? Is it just a matter of persistence – or is it to do with giving ourselves to God's purposes, come what may? Are the two perhaps related together?*

- *Give thanks to God for his generosity.*

PROPER 13

HOSEA 11.1–11

The prophet spoke of a time when the worship of Yahweh alone was far from having a monopoly in Israel: the heritage from Moses was tarnished, and God's faithful love is rejected.

OR ECCLESIASTES 1.2, 12–14; 2.18–23
This is the one book of the Bible which non-believers really approve of! It was written long ago by a top Jerusalem official, world-weary and rather cynical. God hardly comes into his picture, but he does believe in 'wisdom' (i.e. thoughtful competence?) – a decent ideal as far as it goes. But we could aim higher.

COLOSSIANS 3.1–11

At first sight, the passage simply paints the contrast between virtue and vice, good qualities and bad. But Paul's main point is to show how the life of virtue springs straight from the gift of Christ and the impulse that comes to us from him. We do not change ourselves; he changes us, and he is 'all in all'.

LUKE 12.13–21

Here is the answer to the worldly-wise gentleman in Ecclesiastes. Earthly prudence and success are all very well, but they are not the last word, and our hearts had better look further. God is less stuffy than we are.

- *Pray to see that plain good sense is not the last word.*
- *The new life in Christ is the starting point, and virtues follow on.*
- *Where exactly is the snare to be found in riches and what does it mean to be 'rich' towards God?*

PROPER 14

(SUNDAY BETWEEN 7 AND 13 AUGUST INCLUSIVE)

ISAIAH 1.1–10

The prophet takes up his calling in desperate times, with the land either annexed by foreign power or under threat.

OR GENESIS 15.1–6
In Judaism's sense of itself, Abraham is the great father-figure, from whom the whole of Israel has sprung. We may see this as wonderful – and yet restrictive. The picture here is of a beginning, not an end.

HEBREWS 11.1–3, 8–16

Abraham appears in this grand visionary passage as a man of faith. He trusted God when all sense stood against him. Even so, says the writer, still greater things lie in store for us.

LUKE 12.32–40

Expectation, excitement and alertness: these child-like qualities are required of us if we are to be ready for God's astounding generosity to us, summed up in the image of 'the Kingdom'.

- *It is good to be always amazed at the great promise concealed in small things.*

- *In part, 'faith' means simply trust – a disposition rather than a body of beliefs.*

- *Such trust then entails being ready for whatever God asks or gives.*

PROPER 15

(SUNDAY BETWEEN 14 AND 20 AUGUST INCLUSIVE)

ISAIAH 5.1–7

The prophet's poetic utterance combines love with sadness – on behalf of God, whose care for his own is unceasing, but so often met with resistance and infidelity.

OR JEREMIAH 23.23–29
Religious leaders are as liable to deceive (themselves and us) as are other kinds of leaders, and it is not always easy to tell who and what is genuine or wholesome. Jeremiah seems to think that if the message is severe and tough (and therefore unpopular), it is more likely to be the real thing.

HEBREWS 11.29—12.2

This is a passage whose beauty and strength are only spoiled by comment. It depicts Christian confidence without nasty triumphalism, and the sense of having arrived is absolute. It is heartening to take it on board.

LUKE 12.49–56

Jesus and his early followers did not minimize the upset and stir they were causing. 'Family values' were not at the top of their agenda – if they got in the way of the challenge of service to God. Whirlwinds do not stop to consider our instinct for peace and quiet.

- *Pray for the gift of discernment among the clamour of voices that come to us.*

- *Our journey has an end that is assured and we proceed simply 'by faith'.*

- *We shrink from upset and division. But is that always the highest of aims?*

PROPER 16

JEREMIAH 1.4–10

Vocation is a mysterious business, and surprising people can find themselves taking on amazing tasks, sometimes early in life and despite the tut-tuts of others.

OR ISAIAH 58.9–14

A call to give oneself – and one's community – afresh to God. Renewed service of those in need will bring its reward from God, and a new dawn will arise for his people.

HEBREWS 12.18–29

A hard passage to engage with; but its point is to keep us aware of the bewildering mystery and power with which God surrounds us. There is a proper fearfulness and sense of being overwhelmed by what is given to us.

LUKE 13.10–17

Like other stories of healing on the sabbath, this one tells us of Jesus' priorities. Nothing, in the way of rules or conventions, must stand in the way of God's restoring love.

- *The call of God may be no respecter of social good sense. But how can we tell when it is genuine?*

- *We need to hold on to a sense of God's endless mysteriousness, beyond our easy summing up.*

- *Rules may be made to be broken – in the greatest of good causes.*

PROPER 17

JEREMIAH 2.4–13

The prophet's call is consistent. It is to summon the people to renewed
faithfulness to their heritage and God's gifts to them.

OR ECCLESIASTICUS 10.12–18
A reflection on God's powers to dispose the fortunes of nations and to
overthrow those that are consumed by pride.

OR PROVERBS 25.6–7
The ancient world, as witnessed in both Old and New Testaments, was even
more conscious of pecking orders, honour and shame, than we are. It takes an
effort of imagination to feel as acutely as they felt (or perhaps it doesn't?).

HEBREWS 13.1–8, 15–16

The statement about perhaps entertaining angels unawares refers to the story
of the heavenly visitors to Abraham who promise Isaac's birth (Genesis 18).
But it is the words about the utter dependability of Jesus that stay in the mind.

LUKE 14.1, 7–14

This story of musical chairs has a serious point. There is virtue in even the
humdrum exercise of humility – and also in (occasional?) recklessness of
hospitality: it purges the heart and the conscience. A breath of open fresh air,
with a serious point to it.

- *Homely social and courteous gestures can be costly – but also of big
  moral benefit.*

- *What does it mean to take Jesus as the rock we must rely upon?*

- *Behind humility lies genuine 'not caring' about the things that fortify our
  pride.*

PROPER 18

(SUNDAY BETWEEN 4 AND 10 SEPTEMBER INCLUSIVE)

JEREMIAH 18.1–11

The prophet makes a striking demonstration of his message of judgement on God's people and its rules. Only repentance will suffice.

OR DEUTERONOMY 30.15–20

Israel is poised on the point of entry, at long last, into the land of promise. It is a moment of huge seriousness – and of choice. Will she stay faithful to the Giver of all her good?

PHILEMON

Perhaps this brief letter survived because it was precious to a particular person, most likely Onesimus, the slave in whose interest Paul intercedes and whose service he himself needs. Not long after, a man of that name was head of the church in Ephesus, a major Christian centre. A 'maybe' of early Christian history. Paul is shown here at his most attractive.

LUKE 14.25–33

Here is some of the most strident and forbidding teaching in the Gospels. The service of Jesus will be hard; and it is no good cutting corners as we read these words. Can we survive them?

- *The reality and severity of choice, for or against God, faced Israel – and faces us all.*

- *Christian life often boils down to small-scale matters of kindness and help; but even they can be full of spiritual promise.*

- *Attention to individual relationships is among our dearest gifts and basic duties.*

PROPER 19

JEREMIAH 4.11–12, 22–28

One of the prophet's bleakest oracles, uttered in a mood that is without hope of change.

OR EXODUS 32.7–14

The story of the golden calf has become the classic picture of idolatry and falling away from God. And yet God stays faithful. It has its echoes on the levels of both individuals and groups.

1 TIMOTHY 1.12–17

The passage gives the most familiar images, of Paul the persecutor who turned to be an apostle. He saw this as a gift of sheer unmerited grace, and it dominated his faith. He never ceased to sing of it as the pattern of God's loving dealings with us.

LUKE 15.1–10

The main point is clear. But is there a touch of irony in the reference to 'ninety-nine who need no repentance'? If you count yourself among them, you show you haven't got the point – do you not?

- *We reflect on the business of turning to God and being accepted by him.*

- *It is a gift we easily let slip and even abandon.*

- *It is a gift that comes not by our deserving but by his pure generosity. He is relentless in his longing to count us in. Why bother to hide?*

PROPER 20

(SUNDAY BETWEEN 18 AND 24 SEPTEMBER INCLUSIVE)

JEREMIAH 8.18—9.1

The prophet is in despair over the treachery of Israel against God.

OR AMOS 8.4–7
The prophet Amos is notable for his strong message of social justice and protest – against the tricks of the better-off in their exploiting of the poor. And who shall say (and why?) that religion has no bearing on politics?

1 TIMOTHY 2.1–7

This is the earliest example of 'establishment' religion from a Christian voice – and you can almost hear already the Tudor English Prayer Book. It is the other side of the coin from the message of Amos. Christians do have a duty to help construct a stable society, one of the greatest (and most fragile) of all goods. So long as it is just.

LUKE 16.1–13

It is the most obscure and even shocking story of all those told by Jesus. Why exactly is the dishonest man commended? Probably because at least he had the sense to act, in the crisis of his life. Whether we know it or not, we too are in a fix – and need above all to act, and to give ourselves to God's cause.

- *The voice of godly protest is surely to be encouraged, even demanded.*
- *Yet stability is so great a good that it should never be lightly threatened.*
- *And the deepest crisis we face concerns the root of our allegiance. Where does our heart lie?*

PROPER 21

JEREMIAH 32.1–3A, 6–15

The prophet seemed to be nothing less than a traitor when it came to the time of invasion of Judah and the siege of Jerusalem. But he maintained, dramatically, a hope of ultimate redemption.

OR AMOS 6.1A, 4–7

Amos does not like the rich! And who can deny that affluence brings grave moral perils? Never mind, they can be overcome by generosity of heart – and pocket. Simple remedies. Oh dear.

1 TIMOTHY 6.6–19

A passage full of familiar 'quotes'. It plunges us into seriousness – and its sole basis is the example of Jesus, especially his conduct in his Passion. That is where he most plainly discloses God to us and brings us to him.

LUKE 16.19–31

The parable is a picture of extremes. Callous self-indulgence on the one hand, and abject degradation on the other. We are more used to some softening at the edges – though we may not need to go far to find situations pretty close to those in the story. But here, the fault of the rich lies in the hard casing on the conscience: nothing (not even a resurrection) can get through it.

- *Which of us is immune to the battering inflicted in today's readings?*

- *Jesus lived in a largely desperately poor and pitiless society, and we do not. Can we enter the spirit of these words?*

- *How exactly does corruption through affluence bite?*

PROPER 22

(SUNDAY BETWEEN 2 AND 8 OCTOBER INCLUSIVE)

LAMENTATIONS 1.1-6

Grief at the tragedy of Jerusalem's capture by the enemy in 587 BC, here expressed poignantly, has been taken up in relation to the Passion of Jesus when the city failed to grasp its destiny once more.

OR HABAKKUK 1.1-4; 2.1-4

The most memorable words here come at the end. Paul seized on them as the key to his understanding of the gospel.

2 TIMOTHY 1.1-14

Here, in a letter probably by a follower of Paul a few years after his time, we get a picture of Christian faith as an inheritance to be held fast and passed on. The spirit of Paul lives on in those devoted to him.

LUKE 17.5-10

The final sentence puts the lid on all Christian complacency. Our calling is without limits.

- *Pray to find 'life' by the gift of faith.*
- *Thank God for the striking power that can be ours.*
- *Pray that we may do our duty – at least!*

PROPER 23

JEREMIAH 29.1, 4–7

The prophet, speaking to those from Judah now in exile in Babylon, tells them to settle in their new abode peacefully and happily. We have no one abiding city.

OR 2 KINGS 5.1–3, 7–15B

This is a dramatic story, part of a long saga about the deeds of Elijah and Elisha. Its point is to say that the God of Israel extends his compassion beyond Israel's bounds – whatever people of narrower outlook may think right and proper.

2 TIMOTHY 2.8–15

Paul the venerable apostle appears here as the very model of Christian leadership, edifying us by his fidelity and sureness of attachment to his task and role.

LUKE 17.11–19

Luke has a soft spot for the despised Samaritans (seen by the main body of Israel as off-centre, second-grade Jews) – both here in his Gospel and in Acts. It is, as so often, those who are not quite respectable and have no conceit in themselves who are ready to turn towards Christ. They have no pride to hold them back.

- *We should never be too proud to open ourselves to God's generosity and to seeing it freely given.*

- *The solemnity of Paul's words may make us ponder in respectful silence.*

- *God's goodness to us does not depend on our response, but it is right and good when we give it all the same.*

PROPER 24

(SUNDAY BETWEEN 16 AND 22 OCTOBER INCLUSIVE)

JEREMIAH 31.27–34

The disaster of captivity will not be the end and God will be faithful to his people. And then there will be a marvellous new start.

OR GENESIS 32.22–31

It is a mysterious story, one of a number that tell of an encounter between one of us (though a special one) and the holy God (or is that quite who it is?). To Christian readers, it has seemed to point us to our experience of Christ. He can be both clear and yet elusive, among us yet also beyond.

2 TIMOTHY 3.14—4.5

This passage breathes a sense of foreboding, of sad days to come, when Christians will fail to hold to the vision of truth that has been given to them. It is sobering, and we can get its sense all too clearly.

LUKE 18.1–8

Does God really need badgering in this way before he pays attention to us? It is a half-comic tale, meant to urge us to stick to God, through thick and thin.

- *There must always be mystery in our dealings with God. Otherwise, he would simply diminish to our own level.*

- *Faith is never guaranteed from 'going off'; and vigilance is asked of us all.*

- *Part of such vigilance is to persevere in our attentiveness to God despite all discouragements.*

PROPER 25

(SUNDAY BETWEEN 23 AND 30 OCTOBER INCLUSIVE)

JOEL 2.23–32

A message of strong confidence in God. He will stand by his people.

OR ECCLESIASTICUS 35.12–17
The passage reflects the morality of the devout in the ruling class: no corrupt practices and the exercise of true and fair justice.

OR JEREMIAH 14.7–10, 19–22
Times are so bad that the prophet fears that God has given up on his people.

2 TIMOTHY 4.6–8, 16–18

A poignant (and perhaps genuinely Pauline) ending to his letter. It expresses full confidence in God and the fulfilment of hope.

LUKE 18.9–14

This is such a flagrant contrast that only if one were the most extreme of Pharisees (on Luke's model) could one fail to get the point.

- *Pray always to trust God – to the very end.*
- *How strong is our belief in God when adversity strikes?*
- *Paul is a fine example of faith despite all deterrents.*

BIBLE SUNDAY

ISAIAH 45.22–25

The picture is of God like a great king who utters his word – and everybody jumps to obey. He achieves his aims, and we share in his triumph. Confidence is the name of the game.

ROMANS 15.1–6

Paul commends the scriptures of Israel (our Old Testament) as giving us strength and courage, so contributing to our well-being with God.

LUKE 4.16–24

Jesus gives his 'keynote speech' in the synagogue at Nazareth, and, as he reads from Isaiah 61, we hear what amounts to the programme for his mission of rescue and healing and love.

- *We are deluged in words and can easily lose sight of their intrinsic power to form us.*
- *Scripture takes its place among our guides to God.*
- *Does the Nazareth reading sum up Jesus' whole purpose?*

DEDICATION FESTIVAL

(FIRST SUNDAY IN OCTOBER OR LAST SUNDAY AFTER TRINITY)

1 CHRONICLES 29.6–19

In this late version of older history, David the King expresses humility before God, as the building of the Temple in Jerusalem is set in train. All good comes from God alone.

EPHESIANS 2.19–22

The community of God's people is the true bridge between heaven and earth, the place of true holiness, in and through Christ.

JOHN 2.13–22

A passage to stop this festival going over the top! Jesus himself is the true centre of Christian worship, our route to God. All else is secondary.

- *Our offerings to God are themselves his gifts to us.*
- *May worship always centre on God for his own sake alone.*
- *The Church has no reason for its life apart from Christ its centre.*

ALL SAINTS' DAY (1 NOVEMBER)

See Year A, page 65.

ALL SAINTS' SUNDAY

See Year A, page 65.

FOURTH SUNDAY BEFORE ADVENT

ISAIAH 1.10–18

A strident attack by the prophet on the cycle of worship, where virtuous life is not matched to the routine of ritual. It is time to repent.

2 THESSALONIANS 1.1–4 (5–10), 11–12

As often in Paul's letters, we find he begins with warm words, binding the readers to himself and entering into their needs.

LUKE 19.1–10

One of the most attractive of Gospel stories, but in content it is typical of many others. Jesus cuts formality and wins through to the rich tax man, bringing salvation.

- *Pray to shun purely formalized worship.*
- *Thank God for good examples of pastoral care.*
- *We praise God for his gracious welcome of penitent sinners.*

THIRD SUNDAY BEFORE ADVENT

JOB 19.23–27A

Job prays for someone to stand for him before God and vindicate him at last (and Handel's music helps the cause).

2 THESSALONIANS 2.1–5, 13–17

The writer looks to the end of the present age – and to his readers' share in its good outcome.

LUKE 20.27–38

A tough puzzle put to Jesus and answered in its own, not entirely convincing, terms.

- *Relationship with God may involve some unease about the future.*
- *Pray for grace to keep confidence in God's saving love.*
- *What should we do with hard – and perhaps unnecessary – religious questions?*

SECOND SUNDAY BEFORE ADVENT

MALACHI 4.1–2A

We are bidden to look to God's bitter-sweet rounding off of all things –
a belief the Church inherited from old Israel.

2 THESSALONIANS 3.6–13

The letter gets down to basics. Work is a Christian as well as a decent social
duty.

LUKE 21.5–19

Jesus paints a picture of the coming End in the colours available in his day.
He will be faithful to his own.

- · *Pray for a spirit of watchfulness before God.*
- *Concern for our further future does not relieve us of present tasks.*
- *Our goal is the love of God, come what may.*

CHRIST THE KING

See Year A, page 69.

HARVEST FESTIVAL

See Year A, page 70.